2009 Poetry Competition f[...]

YoungWriter[...]

I have a
dream 2009

Words to change the world

Martin Luther King

John Lennon

Poets From Northern England

Edited by Vivien Linton

First published in Great Britain in 2009 by:

 Young**Writers**

Young Writers
Remus House
Coltsfoot Drive
Peterborough
PE2 9JX
Telephone: 01733 890066
Website: www.youngwriters.co.uk

All Rights Reserved
Book Design by Spencer Hart & Tim Christian
© Copyright Contributors 2009
SB ISBN 978-1-84924-500-5

Foreword

'I Have a Dream 2009' is a series of poetry collections written by 11 to 18-year-olds from schools and colleges across the UK and overseas. Pupils were invited to send us their poems using the theme 'I Have a Dream'. Selected entries range from dreams they've experienced to childhood fantasies of stardom and wealth, through to inspirational poems of their dreams for a better future and of people who have influenced and inspired their lives.

The series is a snapshot of who and what inspires, influences and enthuses young adults of today. It shows an insight into their hopes, dreams and aspirations of the future and displays how their dreams are an escape from the pressures of today's modern life. Young Writers are proud to present this anthology, which is truly inspired and sure to be an inspiration to all who read it.

Contents

Upton Hall School, Wirral

Walbottle Campus Technology College, Newcastle upon Tyne

Whitburn CE School, Sunderland

The Poems

They Had A Dream

They had a dream that the whole world would live in harmony
And that religious differences would be forgotten
And that some day, one day, we would all join with Nelson Mandela
And Martin Luther King and say 'Free at last, thank God we are free at last!
Free from the chains of poverty and ill health.

I have a dream that Tatamkuilu Afrika is wrong when he says
'Nothing's changed and things in time will change for the better
For all people that are angry and frustrated and feel abandoned.'

We have a dream that as we watch TV
And witness the desperate struggles of childbearing mothers in Malawi
Who do not have the benefits of our health facilities –
That they will one day be able to receive the health benefits we receive
And there will be a better chance for Malawi mothers
To survive the horrors of Aids, childbearing and poverty.

We have a dream like Nelson Mandela
That democracy will be the standard for every country to aspire to
That employment will be available to all
Black, white, mixed race and that the recession in 2009
Will not lead to depression in 2010 for families and bread winners alike.

Megan Wetherell (12)

I Have A Dream

M y dream is to play for Liverpool or England
Y outh team would be better for me to get scouted

D uring my time I would like to play for the Under 18s Liverpool team
R etire at the age of thirty or more
E ither Liverpool or England
A ny team like Liverpool or England would be good
M y dream is to play up front or right wing.

Jake McCarthy (14)
Branksome School, Darlington

1

I Have A Dream

Dreams can be amazing
Beautiful and bright
Dreams can be real or sometimes alive
Sometimes you wish they would come true
And sometimes you need to think them
Through and through.

Dreams can be horrid
Upsetting and bad
Dreams can sometimes make you sad
Nightmare and fright
When you're asleep at night
Your imagination messes with your head
I bet you just wish you could be in bed.

From little to old
Dreams go and go
You could want to do football
Or sing in a hall
You could want to write books
Or even have nip 'n' tuck.

Family or business
It's all your choice
Some dreams are true
But then go away
Just think about being a chef
And cooking dreams
Or being a gardener
They're all parts of dreams.

Beth Hunter (14)
Branksome School, Darlington

I Have A Dream

I have a dream to drive a Lamborghini Gallardo one day and in the
colour orange
This is because I have a lot of interest in cars
And a lot of potential in passing my driving on my first ever attempt.
I want to have a relaxing job, with a well paid salary
And not only that but the colleagues to be friendly as well
And then I can think at least I can trust someone to talk to.
I have a dream to go to university
And get a good education out of my life
Not only that, because then you have something to feel proud about
inside you.
I have a dream to leave this school with good GCSE levels
So that my family feels proud of me.
Not only that, I am thinking about my future and how I'm going to run my life
And so it's for my future, to live a good life with some freedom as well.

Ashraf Ahmed Alavi (14)
Branksome School, Darlington

I Have A Dream

I love to play football

H aving fun with my friends at training

A nd my dream is to become a professional footballer

V ery important that I stick at training

E very training session I need to show my skill

A nd the most important thing is not to take drugs or drink alcohol

D ay in and day out I think of becoming a professional

R eally good, I want to be at the top of my game

E nd of the day I go to bed and dream to play for Newcastle

A nd someday it might come true

M ight, might not come true as I want it too!

Lewis Stockill (14)
Branksome School, Darlington

I Have A Dream

I have a dream that I think about
Also you could think of it as sometimes special
Could be something amazing, something you've wanted for ages
Could be as small as you wanted
It will still be your dream till you get it
You still wish for this dream and it could come true one day
My dream is that I could be famous one day, maybe once
It could come true one time or one day
Might come true, once in your life
Still dreaming and it might come
It could be amazing, great and absolutely good
People might not want to be famous but I do
Could be famous is a good thing
This life with fame could be a good life
And I could be having a great time!

Carla Diaper (13)
Branksome School, Darlington

I Have A Dream

I have a dream to go into the Olympics.
I have a dream to go into the 2012 Olympics.
I have a dream to win the 2012 Olympics.
I have a dream to be the world's greatest gymnast.
I have a dream . . .

Craig Pearson (13)
Branksome School, Darlington

Dream, Dream, Dream

I have a dream
A dream that might come true
Very important for me
It might not be very important to you
My dream is to manage a team
Take them and win the World Cup
I'll bring Rooney and Lampard
Terry and Gerrard
My dream is to manage England
Until I live the dream, the dream will live on
But when I die, that dream will be gone.

Paul Cooper (14)
Branksome School, Darlington

Dream Come True

I have a dream that I would travel all around the world.
I have a dream that I would see all the amazing stuff around the world.
I have a dream that I would get a bit out of everything and everywhere
I visit.
I have a dream that one day I could do all those things and live my dream.
This is my dream, what is yours?

Hamida Begum (13)
Branksome School, Darlington

I Had A Dream

I had a dream
That I was sixteen
I was up and down
Left to right
Then I was told to get out of sight.

I had a dream
That I was fifteen
Fed up with life
Then I got a fright
And then I got ice cream.

I had a dream
That I was fourteen
I got up for school
Became a fool
And then I got a fright.

I had a dream
That I was thirteen
I was sure to get a fright
But on that day I had to play
And then I was quite all right.

Then I woke
I realised I was ninety
What a big fright I got!

Christopher Mordue (12)
Churchill Community College, Wallsend

Freedom, Liberty, Equality

Freedom is not a guaranteed right of humanity
But a hard and brutal odyssey of independence and self-liberation
A search for equality and common moral standing for every man, woman
and child
A fight of sacrifice and reward, of defeat and victory, oppression and
freedom.

I stand before you a free man, for I have sacrificed for my freedom and
together
We shall cast off the shackles of our oppressors
We shall make them bleed for we shall bleed no more.
We shall walk free without fear
We shall forge the cradle of freedom and liberty through our sacrifice.

Fight for your freedom, fight for your liberty, fight for your equality
Let me tell you, we shall be free.

For there is no limit to what we can achieve,
There is no limit to what we will achieve.

Matthew Thirlaway (15)
Churchill Community College, Wallsend

A Dream Of Being Me

I dream of a world with love,
I dream of a world with hope,
I dream of a world with acceptance,
I dream of a world that can cope.

I dream of a life with equality,
I dream of a life with care,
I dream of a life with ability,
I dream there's always someone there.

I dream of many different things
That I wish were upon this Earth.
So there is a meaning to every hopeful prayer
And a meaning to every birth.

Yes, many have a dream of love
And of equality.
But I possess the strongest of all
My dream is being me.

Victoria Strachan (15)
Churchill Community College, Wallsend

My Dream

Children lie awake wondering how they will survive
With no close relatives to help their lives
They should be tucked up in their beds
With hopes and dreams inside their heads
Now they are thinking of food and drink
When they should be learning how to think
Working hard for little pay
While fortunate ones are thinking of what to say
Coughing, sneezing, with no one to care
Other children with family there
How will they cope?
Their lives will get better, I hope.

Ellen Reynolds (14)
Dame Allan's Girls' School, Newcastle upon Tyne

I Have A Dream

Dreams, aspirations, passions,
Things that direct and affect our life.
Feelings which inspire and motivate,
The blank paper of our life,
With which we are born
Can be affected by the way we hold our pens
Held aloft,
Catching the beads of inspiration and adding them to the collection
Any order, any direction
Etched onto the surface
Only the firm and deep ink can last
You take care of your dreams and let them breathe
Taste the air around you and find they can move
Dancing around in the light, never stopping
Leading me forward, helping me shine too
These things I have wanted
Soaring above the trees
Falling upon the ears of kindly people
That can help me on my way.
To go down in history and be forever remembered
On stage and screen, underneath the lights
With family and friends that have never been forgotten
All together on my roller coaster of life
Here I realise
Dreams are feelings
No matter how big
No matter how small that come from your heart
Made into reality by dedicated actions
And that's how it goes
My happily ever after my dream.

Amy Lyall (14)
Dame Allan's Girls' School, Newcastle upon Tyne

I Had A Dream

People were speaking, crying and screaming,
Nothing was there and her tears began streaming.
I tugged on my hair, my eyes shut to think,
Her forehead was throbbing and her face turned deep pink.
I knelt to the gourd and cried to the sky,
'Oh come on Lord, come on God, please why?'
She wretched, threw up blood and passed out with a yelp
I knew she was dying, I needed some help.
My best friend forever was leaving the world
I wanted her back and I nearly hurled.
I put my ear to her chest and sputtered, 'Oh no!'
Her heart, it just fluttered, no, please just don't go!
She lifted her arm and clawed at the air
I screeched out, I'm here, as sweat dripped from her hair.
I won't let you go, I swore, crossed my heart
But even just now I felt us drifting apart.
She snatched up my hand and whispered, 'start over my friend,'
'I'm not starting anything! I'm here till the end.'
She spoke her last words of which there were few
'I'm dying; I love you and will miss you too,'
She slumped on the pillow; her heart thumped its last
I held her and screamed and hugged her like a cast
'No, you're not gone!' I touched her cold cheek
I went to my house, stayed there for many a week.
But even now after all of these years
I still remember back and remember that girl
And she is still a major part
A part of my world.

Rosie Douglas (14)
Dame Allan's Girls' School, Newcastle upon Tyne

I Have A Dream

I sleep in the clouds and dream life away
In my castle in the air I will always stay
Life flutters by as I gaze down below
As I watch the sun rising with a welcoming glow

A dream is a dream whether minor or great
And like life itself, the ending is fate
Myself down on Earth, myself in the sky
Living and dreaming from now till I die.

My thoughts appear to keep me sane
As I consider a life without fear or pain
I know life's worth living, no matter what comes your way
To wake up not knowing what'll happen each day.

Clouds surround me as I soar up high
Dreaming of pleasures right there in the sky
I sleep in the clouds and dream life away
In my castle, in the air, I will always stay.

Ruby Lawson (13)
Dame Allan's Girls' School, Newcastle upon Tyne

I Have A Dream

I have a dream to be
As successful as anyone would want to be
To travel where anyone would want to travel
To experience what others would love to experience.

I have a dream to achieve
What I want to achieve
To be as worthy as anybody
To live the way I want to live.

I have a dream to become
Become what I choose
To enjoy what I choose to become
To be someone who enjoys what I have become.

Kathryn Woolston-Thomas (14)
Dame Allan's Girls' School, Newcastle upon Tyne

Hunting Animals Poem

Imagine if you were that creature getting killed
Feeling the pain and torture done to you
If they continued this to you, you wouldn't be chilled
If you were captured, you wouldn't have the chance to go to the loo.
Pretend if they took your homes out
And they caged you in a cell
Your owner would yell and shout
You were so sad and depressed, everyone could tell.

You were so happy when you were in the wild
Playing happily with your family and friends
You were so calm and mild
But in this jail, you won't be able to twist and bend.

Please stop this torture and torment
You would save lots of money and a creature's life.
Imagine if you were in a burning tent
You would be in so much pain; you would call for your wife.

Uzair Oomer (13)
Essa Academy, Bolton

Child Abuse

It's time for bed, everyone is asleep, I can't close my eyes
Wondering if he'll come again, I keep twisting and turning
He's hurt me.

I want to tell my mummy but I'm scared,
She wouldn't care anyway, she loves Daddy more than me.
I hear a crack,
I can feel the tears at the back of my eyes,
He comes into my room stinking of booze
I ask him softly, 'Daddy, are you OK?' He doesn't reply
He tells me to take my clothes off, I feel like I'm going to die.

I'm shaking with fright, he grabs me really tight.
I know what he's going to do,
I can't bear the pain,
He tries to come closer, but I push him away.
I scream for help
But he pushes the pillow across my mouth.
I can't breathe, I can't breathe but finally he lets go.
I run for the door, but he's locked it shut.
I think, *why does this happen to me?*
Again, he tells me to pull my clothes off,
This time I cry.
I hear footsteps . . .

It's Mum, she's knocking on my door
Daddy tells me to keep quiet about everything, how?
She comes in and asks why my eyes are red
Dad replies, I fell and hurt myself, he came to comfort me
I want to tell her the truth, I really do.

But if I'm saved today, I won't be tomorrow
My story will never have an end
Some kids wish they had parents, I wish, I didn't.

Mubasshera Patel (13)
Essa Academy, Bolton

13

Child Abuse

Child abuse is many things
Each one as bad as the other
Each type can lead to death.

Neglect can lead to dehydration
Hypothermia and starvation
Violence can lead to homicide
Or a child committing suicide.

Constantly putting a child down
Can make them feel pathetic
Stupid and worthless
It can cause them to kill themselves.

Sexual abuse can cause
A child to cry and cry
And that can result in suicide.

If any of this happens to you
Don't let the person continue
Tell someone you can trust
And they'll make you safe.

They'll make you feel stronger
And the abuse won't last any longer
Because your abuser will be taken away from you
And all the suffering will stop.

So if we all work together
We can stop this forever
And children can be happy and safe.
Stop it now!

Katie Crompton (13)
Essa Academy, Bolton

Stop Knife!

Murder, murder, murder,
The Earth will come to an end.
Murder, murder, murder,
If your worst enemy or friend.
Murder, murder, murder,
It's only a knife.
Murder, murder, murder,
That takes an innocent life.

Murder, murder, murder,
You will get caught!
Murder, murder, murder,
But it takes out a lot of thought.
Murder, murder, murder,
Why are we doing this?
Murder, murder, murder,
All the friends and family will be sadly missed.

Murder, murder, murder,
Stop this stupid nonsense.
Murder, murder, murder,
You and your guilty conscience.
Murder, murder, murder,
Give yourself up before it's too late.
Murder, murder, murder,
It's either love or hate.

Don't use a knife
It's either yours or someone else's life.

Ashley Hayes (13)
Essa Academy, Bolton

Anorexic, Am I?

It's dinnertime
Mummy passes me the plate
Tell her I've already ate
I think to myself, if I have no dinner, I'll be much thinner

It's evening now, Mummy's made my favourite
Shepherd's pie
I try not to cry
She knocks on my door
I'm still on the floor.

I'm forced to eat
I miss out the meat
Now she's gone, I try to make myself sick
I succeed but people take the Mick

I can't control it
Sometimes I have a fit
People say I'm mentally ill
I'm empty
I need to be filled

I need help now
I need help but how?
I tell my doctor Tim
I trust him
He says he will be here
It's very near.

Faizah Ahmed (13)
Essa Academy, Bolton

Global Warming Poem!

You may say that it's science fiction
But we know global warming is a scientific fact which cannot be denied.
If we work together we can fight back
But if we work separately, there are lots of things we'll lack.

Fossil fuels are burnt on a daily basis
If we carry on not distracted like this
We'll regret it and it will show on our faces.
But if we reduce our carbon footprint we will be saved
And we won't be a victim of our own faults and also, we won't become our
own slaves.

Global warming can easily turn into an ice age if we continue like this
We'll be stuck in our own cold steel cage
Global warming means the icebergs melting which will be dumped into the
ocean
And stop the ocean conveyer
And we'll lose our last surviving layer.
There are many ways we can stop this cruel fate and one way is recycling
If we all work together we can all contribute
It's a dream that will be fulfilled
I've only got a few more words to say: our future, it's in our hands.

Rizwaan Lakhi (12)
Essa Academy, Bolton

Bullies

I wake up, I pray
That school will be different today
As I was bullied yesterday
And as I walk up to the gate
I see that boy who I hate.
He hits me, he calls me
He makes me feel sick but yet I still take it
I try and tell the teacher but every time I try
He always hits me in the eye
And yet I still try not to cry

I see him here, I see him there
He makes me feel so scared
But why, oh why, should I be scared
As he's only a boy just like me

He walks like me, he talks like me
He even dresses like me
So why does he still hate me?

William Adamson (13)
Essa Academy, Bolton

Stop Taking Drugs!

Stop taking drugs!
It's a risk you shouldn't take
You can lose your life
It's not a success you will make
So stop taking drugs!

Stop taking drugs!
It's a very painful death
You might enjoy taking them now
But you won't with the rest
So stop taking drugs!

Stop taking drugs!
Crack, weed, ecstasy or heroine
All of these will lead to prison
Two years, five years or all of your time
Any one of these will ruin your life
So stop taking drugs!

Juwairiya Vaid (12)
Essa Academy, Bolton

Black Or White

It's not about colour or creed
Not the money, not the greed
No wars, no fights
Everything is set right.

Shoot a guy, day or night,
It was never about black or white
Take somebody's life
Shoot him or kill him with a knife.

Fallen soldier, fallen troop
Like jumping through a fire on a hoop
Taking your life
Think of your kids and wife.

Nizam Giga (13)
Essa Academy, Bolton

19

Money, Money, Money

There are a lot of people with more money than they need,
They've been taken over by something called greed.
They have so much money that's in the bank to spend,
Just to use it to get into the new fashion trend.
They want shoes, cars and clothing,
Plus that useless bling Bling!
There are people in the world that need this money,
However these stupid rich people think it's funny.
They live on the street or small huts they made,
They do their work but still don't get paid.
In one country in Africa
Over thirty kids die from malaria.
So what you should do is give to charity,
1p to £10, anything is enough,
You only lose a little but they gain a lot.

Adil Mbarushimana (13)
Essa Academy, Bolton

I Have A Dream

I have a dream
That one day all the people in the wars
Will come together and make peace.
I have a dream
That poverty will be no longer.
I have a dream
That our country will have no problems
With people from other countries
So they can come to our country.
I have a dream
That religions will come together.
I have a dream
That one day I will become a professional rugby player
And that my family will have peace.

Joshua Garbett (13)
Fleetwood Sports College, Fleetwood

Open Your Eyes

Sitting in front of a candle
Watching as the flame burns out
Lost hope
Extinguished so quickly with a single breath.

I sit and wonder
Wonder why we're living life in half view
Afraid to look into the eyes of a stranger we all know so well.

I wonder what love is
And when it went away.

And I fight
No armour to cover my torso
There's no hiding here.

I am fighting for life.

Life where people are not afraid to cross over the road
Where we may love, laugh and live like there's no tomorrow
Where we may let our colours shine.

I cannot pick up the pieces of society alone.
I ask you to open your eyes
Everything that matters is right in front of you
Discrimination must be overthrown by determination.

We are one,
We are the world.

Open your eyes.

Beth Malam (13)
Fleetwood Sports College, Fleetwood

21

Change

I think about the changes
Watching clouds go by.
If people don't stop dropping
The world will just start rotting.
There'll be no fields to run wild
Running like a little child.
There'll be no seas, no ocean blue,
Sea creatures all gone too.
There'll be no life, no bees, no trees,
No children sat on parents' knees.
There'll be no people,
No Earth at all.
If we were like all other creatures
Our world would be pure and simple
But we're not and if we don't change our ways
Our world will die.
So the humans of our planet
Have a very simple choice
No litter or no life!

Josephine Andrews (12)
Fleetwood Sports College, Fleetwood

I Have A Dream

In the future I dream that there are no drugs
I dream that there will be no animal rugs
I dream that all the wars will end
I dream that everyone could be friends
I dream that people aren't cruel to their pets
In the future I dream to be a vet
I dream to live my life healthy
I dream to be wealthy
I dream to have a nice car
I dream that my dreams will take me far.

Rebecca Hind (12)
Fleetwood Sports College, Fleetwood

22

I Have A Dream

Imagine
A safe world
Imagine
No bullying
Imagine
No drugs
Imagine
No violence
Imagine
No wars
Imagine
Getting a brilliant job
Imagine
No smoking
Imagine
A safer world
Imagine
Living my life without any danger in the world.

Jack Long (12)
Fleetwood Sports College, Fleetwood

What Would The World Be Like?

What would the world be like . . .
If the devastating murders of terrorism finished?
If the life-stealing poverty came to an end?
If the mind-blowing wars came to a halt?
If the amazing creatures were not killed?
If the religions were happy with everyone else
If the sadness of murder and suicides stopped?
If the people were all treated the same?
If everyone was happy with everyone around them?
If we could live in peace together?

Samantha Eykyn (13)
Fleetwood Sports College, Fleetwood

Just Think

Think about what the world dreams of,
Think about what they want,
Think about if their dreams could be important,
Think about what they could do,
Think about if there was world peace,
Think about what it would be like.
Think about walking down the road and not being called names,
Think about being treated the same,
Think about how you would feel,
Think about growing up in harmony,
Think about what we could do,
Think about what we could become if everyone was supportive instead of
                                              knocking us back,
Think about no guns,
Think about other things we could use,
Think about hugs and kisses and making friends instead,
Think about how it would make the world feel,
Think about how it would make you feel.

Natalie Knibbs (12)
Fleetwood Sports College, Fleetwood

I Had A Dream

I had a dream that all heroic wars would be eradicated.
I had a dream that everyone in the universe could fly.
I had a dream that all pollution would vanish.
I had a dream that each and every creature could talk.
I had a dream the world would be in peace.
I had a dream that I could rule the world.
I had a dream that superpowers would exist.
I had a dream that everyone had a proper home.
I had a dream that I won one thousand pounds.
I had a dream that all my dreams came true.

Daryll Rankine (13)
Fleetwood Sports College, Fleetwood

I Dream From The Heart

I dream that one day my voice will be heard.
I dream that I can cut the tension between all races with the scissors
of freedom.
I dream that the planet will be treated with respect, treated with kindness.
This planet gives us life, let's give it back.
I dream for everlasting peace, no wars,
Only fight for the freedom we can achieve if we put our minds to it.
I dream to quench the thirsty, home the homeless
And to let the stomachs be full in every unique being.
I dream for OAPs to all have an equal share in pensions
And to not feel intimidated by others.
I dream for everyone to play the same song on the guitar of life.
I dream for everyone to be equal, nobody to feel intimidated or threatened.
I dream for the utopia that we can create
If we stop arguing for no reason and concentrate.
I dream for my voice to be heard.

Chris Pook (13)
Fleetwood Sports College, Fleetwood

This Is My Dream

I have a dream
A dream that every war and violent conflict will end.
I am passionate about this dream
And I'm sure if it happens,
No more dreams will be needed.
My dream, my dream can be your dream,
Just imagine, imagine this as a nightmare
No one would be safe.
Lives of loved ones saved is my dream
My dream has different perspectives
A perspective where everyone is safe
Everyone can live knowing they've loved.
This is my dream.

Joel Khambay (13)
Fleetwood Sports College, Fleetwood

25

I Have A Dream

I have a dream,
A dream that all wars will stop
And the awful crying of starving
Children desperate for food will too.

I have a dream,
The world will be in peace
And the beautiful trees will blow in harmony.

I have a dream,
That the creatures of the Earth
Will be able to talk to tell us how they feel.

I have one more dream I hope to share,
That when I become older I shall be a vet
And my grandad will be alive.

I have a dream!

Charlotte Helsby (13)
Fleetwood Sports College, Fleetwood

I Have A Dream

I have a dream
For war to stop
I have a dream
For no more racism
I have a dream
For a greener world
I have a dream
For no more smoking
I have a dream
To be a rugby player
I have a dream
For a new pair of boots
I have a dream
For a happier world.

Daniel Shuttleworth (11)
Fleetwood Sports College, Fleetwood

I Have A Dream

I have a dream . . .
A life with no pain and suffering,
A life which our ancestors longed for,
A life where everything is good and pure.

I have a dream . . .
Where I stand in front of hundreds and inspire and influence,
Where I change generations,
Where I help young people and their violent ways.

I have a dream . . .
For Man to take care of and appreciate our planet,
For everyone to be equal and no discrimination,
For peace on Earth.

Sammy Haugan (11)
Fleetwood Sports College, Fleetwood

I Have A Dream

In the future I dream no more drugs will be spread around the world.
I have a dream; in the future I dream there will be no more murders
                                              in Fleetwood.
Imagine if someone invented seven-wheeled cars.
Imagine that there could be a cure for all serious injuries for people who get
                                              seriously hurt.
In the future I dream to be a hairdresser.
In the future I dream that there will be enough money in the world to
                                              stop poverty
And all poor people and countries have food, water and a place to live.

Bobby-Leigh Campbell (11)
Fleetwood Sports College, Fleetwood

27

I Have A Dream

I have a dream that all poverty Will end and their lives will be better
than ours.
I have a dream that war will stop and they can come to peace with their
friends and family.
I have a dream that there will be enough money in the world for more
people to get more jobs.
I have a dream that this world will be safer for our children.
I have a dream that everyone will be treated the same.
I have a dream that my family and I will live a long and happy life.

Nicole Oliver (13)
Fleetwood Sports College, Fleetwood

My Dream

I have a dream that violence will stop and bring peace to the world and
nobody will cry.
I have a dream that child abuse will drop and has never happened,
Like fresh air has taken it away.
I have a dream that slavery will drop and vanish into ash from the beaming
hot sun.
I have a dream that bullying will stop
And people will start taking education seriously and take part.
Then I woke up and thought my dreams had come true.

Michael Williams (12)
Fleetwood Sports College, Fleetwood

I Have A Dream

I had a dream that I was in the army saving the world for the war.
I had a dream it would stop and the world would get along.
If it did this, there would be no more violence, slavery or child abuse.
I had a dream it didn't stop because the world is falling apart!
I had a dream you would help, is it true?

Lewis Jones (11)
Fleetwood Sports College, Fleetwood

I Have A Dream

In the future I dream that the world will be better, cleaner, no war and
no poverty.
In the future I dream that my mum will get better from her leukaemia.
In the future I dream that my dad will lose his diabetes and asthma.
In the future I dream that my brother Jordan will lose his asthma.
In the future I dream that we will be closer to my family then we are now.
In the future I dream, I dream, I dream.

Hayley Barker (12)
Fleetwood Sports College, Fleetwood

I Have A Dream

I have a dream that drugs will stop.
I have a dream that violence would drop.
I have a dream of new rules of speeding on the road.
I have a dream of more education and how it will go.
I have a dream about football, which is me.
I have a dream it was meant to be.

Jordan Anderton (12)
Fleetwood Sports College, Fleetwood

I Have A Dream

Children dream:
They dream of a world with no war,
They dream of a world with no bullying,
They dream of a world with no violence,
They dream of a world with no racism,
I have a dream to be a vet.

Emma Jones (11)
Fleetwood Sports College, Fleetwood

Dream The Future

I have a dream to extinguish the fires of war,
I have a dream to stop racism in all its forms.
I have a dream for equality for all,
I have a dream that no good man will fall.
I have a dream to change the world,
I have a dream just to be heard.

Elliott Musgrave (13)
Fleetwood Sports College, Fleetwood

I Have A Dream

I have a dream that bullying will stop.
I have a dream to save those people from slavery.
I have a dream that I could see the floor on the street.
I have a dream that people could see that other people aren't a joke.
I have a dream for all of this to stop.

Stacey Worthington (12)
Fleetwood Sports College, Fleetwood

I Have A Dream

I have a dream that all wars will stop and poverty will be no longer
That the country will not be racist to people who are a different colour to us.
I have a dream that my uncle is not dead and that he can come back to life.
I have a dream that I will become a professional footy player.

Alex Trushell (13)
Fleetwood Sports College, Fleetwood

Crime, Fight It

C   rime, the world is in crisis every minute, every hour, every day
       Is there anything we can do? We can fight it!
R   obber, robber, stop that thief!
       Who will help? No one in the street
I   nnocent people, people extorted for money
       Beaten or tortured, cruel and sick but to thieves it is funny
M   urder, murder every day, we can't just sit here
I   t will never just go away if we live in fear
E   veryone together we can make it stop
       Come on, pitch in, become a cop
F   ighting crime is not a glorious pleasure
       It comes with pain and hardship put together
I   t   's my dream to be a policeman
       With the aspiration to help all good humans
G   reat, small, black and white, it doesn't matter to me
       As long as all people are given a life that is free
H   elping those who dearly need it
       We will truly bring a sense of fulfilment
T   o keep order at every turn
       It would be something I need to learn
I   f over time my dream was fulfilled and I became a cop
       Not all crime would be stopped, but
T   o think I will be helping people in so many ways
       It would enlighten me for the rest of my days.

Allan Lambert (12)
Heworth Grange Comprehensive School, Gateshead

She Has A Dream

She comes from a background of abuse and hurt
Unable to live a normal life
Scared of what will happen now she has put a foot wrong
'Please Daddy, it hurts,' she is screaming and shouting
Trying to escape
She wishes she had never been born
She can't take anymore
She has a dream.

Going to school,
Trying to hide those bruises of that person who doesn't care
She can't tell anyone
She just can't
It will make it all worse
But she is determined
It will get out
She will not let it lie.

Years later she is free, living her dream
Standing up for what she believes
She never will give in
Abuse is wrong, abuse is wrong
She will stop this
She knows how it hurts.

Megan Collins (12)
Heworth Grange Comprehensive School, Gateshead

I Had A Dream

I had a dream I would be like George Sampson
He is amazing at break dancing
He did flips and slides, he also did freezes
He won 'Britain's Got Talent' and blew everyone away
But one day I will be like George Sampson
I have a dream, a very big dream.

Kayne McGillan-Agar (12)
Heworth Grange Comprehensive School, Gateshead

I Have A Dream

I have a dream of no fighting,
Of no people being abused on a football pitch.
It doesn't matter if you're black or white,
Fat or thin, tall or titch.

I have a dream of no more wars,
Of no more people dying,
Of no more murders.
But of people living
To be free and flying.

I have a dream
Of a peaceful world,
Of a world full of natural things
Like flowers
And trees
And human beings.

I have a dream
Of helpful people,
Of people who are kind and caring,
Of children doing well in school.
Helping out
And always sharing.

Charlotte Semmence (12)
Heworth Grange Comprehensive School, Gateshead

I Have A Dream!

I have a dream to play football for England like the great Alan Shearer or
Steven Gerrard.
I have a dream to be brave and fearless like the bold Winston Churchill and
others alike.
I have a dream to conquer my fears and never be afraid again.
I have a dream to become rich and famous for people to know my name
wherever I go.

Thomas Curtis (12)
Heworth Grange Comprehensive School, Gateshead

33

That Is My Dream

Of all the people it could be
Marie Curie inspires me
To be like her and change the world
That is my dream.

Of all the things she has done
The cancer research is my favourite one
I want to help the sick and poorly too
That is my dream.

She spent her time curing the ill
She did this out of her goodwill
She inspired lots of people worldwide
That is my dream.

Marie Curie is my hero
The chances of her giving up were zero
She won two Nobel prizes
That is my dream.

She saved thousands of lives
Most of them survived
I hope to carry on her work
That is my dream.

Caitlin Willis (12)
Heworth Grange Comprehensive School, Gateshead

I Have A Dream

I have an aspiration
Of being a world famous cook.
I always follow the recipe
And always go by the book.

Jamie Oliver is my hero
His food, it looks so great.
Some day my food will be like his
But I guess I'll have to wait.

I dream of doing something awesome
With different foods and drink.
But if I do not practice
My dreams will begin to shrink.

So I have to keep my dreams big
And never give up hope.
I have to keep on fighting
Keep climbing up the slope.

So I really, really want to be
A great and wonderful cook.
For I always follow the recipe
And always go by the book.

Adam Gray (12)
Heworth Grange Comprehensive School, Gateshead

I Have A Dream

My hero is Steve Urwin
He saved crocs all of his life
He got stabbed by a stingray
Its tail was like a knife.

That was the end of his career
And my life long dream
To work with Steve himself
The best keeper I'd ever seen.

I still want to see some Aussies
And see a wild kangaroo
Then maybe even work there
At Australia Zoo.

I cannot work with Steve
As he has passed away
But I will still think of him
Each and every day.

I will not forget my hero
And what he always said
Like, 'Crikey, she's a wopper!'
And 'Take its tail and not its head!'

Ross Drape (12)
Heworth Grange Comprehensive School, Gateshead

A Week Of Sports

I have a dream that I could be a sportsman
Or a sports coach or manager.
Each day I'll do a different sport,
Every week the sports will change.

This week, on Monday, I'll play cricket
Race in a F1 Ferrari and ski slalom.

On Tuesday I'll play darts and manage Spain.
Bungee jump from a mountain and teach bungee jumping as well.

On Wednesday I'll swim the channel and play rugby for France.
Present 'A Question of Sport' show.
A mental sports show and a physical one as well.

On Thursday I'll run a football club, a rugby club
And a snowboarding club and a fancy dress football day.

On Friday I'll go ten pin bowling
Play archery, ski down a mountain and win a tennis trophy.

Then I'll be tired, tired, tired.

James Routledge (13)
Heworth Grange Comprehensive School, Gateshead

Steve Irwin – I Have A Dream

S teve was his name
T erri was his wife
E njoyable programmes he made
V ery exciting life he had
E xtremely dangerous animals he looked after

I rwin was his surname
R escuing animals was what he did
W ild animals he loved
I nteresting, brave and funny he was
N ever to be forgotten.

Scott Dixon (11)
Heworth Grange Comprehensive School, Gateshead

Winston Churchill

W inston Churchill was his name
I n London he resided
N icknamed the British Bulldog
S moked cigars he did
'T o war,' he declared
O nly because Germany attacked Poland
'N o,' he said, 'This cannot happen.'

C hurchill is who I look up to
H e commanded Britain in World War II
U nbelievable his actions were I thought
R ight, he always was and very honourable
C hurchill was also a painter, an artist with great work
H e served as a solder in World War I at the Western Front
'I n every area possible we will fight,' he called during his great speech
L ondon was his home, he defended it with the blood of his people
L eader of the UK, he lead us through World War II.

Connor Dalrymple (12)
Heworth Grange Comprehensive School, Gateshead

I Have A Dream

I have a dream to be like my mum and dad.

H owever sometimes I don't want to be like them
A spirations are something I would like to achieve
V iolence is one of the things I would like to stop
E ventually I want to make these dreams come true.

A spire is what I say when I want to do something.

D reams are all of these things
R un after your dreams like I will
E ventually I want to play the saxophone like my sister
A nd also my sister inspires me
M y dreams are all of these things.

Brittany Willis (11)
Heworth Grange Comprehensive School, Gateshead

I Have A Dream

I have a dream
A very big dream
Where the world has changed
No fighting and no bullying
Just nice people all around.

I have a dream
A very big dream
Where nobody is poor
No tramps and no beggars
Just happy people all around.

I have a dream
A very big dream
Where nobody is racist
No black or white people
Just friendly people all around.

Charlotte Menham (12)
Heworth Grange Comprehensive School, Gateshead

I Have A Dream

J ane Tomlinson inspires me
A ll her effort she gave for all the money she raised
N o one could be a bigger inspiration
E ven though she had cancer she still kept going and running races

T ick-tock the clock was ticking, every second she had, she used
O ther people she thought of even more than she thought of herself
M any people supported her along the way
L oved she was by all her family and friends
I have a dream to run the London Marathon, she is my role model
N ever did she give up, she just kept going
S ix months she was given to live but seven years she battled the disease
O ver and over again she proved them wrong
N ow Jane has died but her inspiration will never be forgotten.

Abbie Calder (12)
Heworth Grange Comprehensive School, Gateshead

I Have A Big Dream

I   have a dream of goodness.

H and out goods to
A ll the poor people in the world
V ery good luck
E njoy your life

A ll the poor people in the world

B oys and girls help your mam
I n good time and bad
G ood is always the answer

D o your jobs
R ead your books
E ven do your homework
A nyway if you are good you
M ight become fortunate one day.

Sean Rowell (12)
Heworth Grange Comprehensive School, Gateshead

I Have A Dream

I   have a dream

H owever other dreams come to mind
A nd I think if I achieve one would I wish to rewind?
V oices in my head tell me which route to take
E ven though one stands out, I don't want to make a mistake

A nd they are all different in many a way

D oesn't matter about the total of my pay
R eward isn't always the best
E ven if I'm rich one day, I don't want my dream to be a pest
A dream as a torture, how would that seem
M aybe I will never achieve any of my dreams!

Clare McGill (12)
Heworth Grange Comprehensive School, Gateshead

I Have A Dream

I have a dream to be a footballer like the skilful Ronaldo and the
powerful Gerrard,
To play for Newcastle United.
If I'm not a footballer, I would like to be a manager,
I'd manage lots of great clubs all around the world like Barcelona and
Liverpool and Newcastle.
I go to football matches, I have heard of lots of legends who have played for
the club I love.
I have a dream that there is no bullying and no fighting and no racism
Because nearly every day I hear a group of people bullying black people,
It makes me feel unhappy.
I have a dream to make everyone in the world happy.
I have a dream that everyone is loved.
I have a dream to own a mansion and own a Bugatti and lots of other
fast cars.

Lee Jaretzke (13)
Heworth Grange Comprehensive School, Gateshead

I Have A Very Special Dream

I have a dream

H ow I want to be a gymnast
A s I practice every night
V arious routines I have made
E very competition I participate

A nd in each one, I get a good place

D reams can come true and hopefully mine will
R acing to victory
E verybody cheers me on
A nd it really boosts my confidence
M y dream, a gymnast.

Rebecca De Cristofaro (12)
Heworth Grange Comprehensive School, Gateshead

Changing The World

I have a dream to change the world
To stop fighting and crime
And to even turn back time
To stop bullying and calling names
It's not funny, it's not a game
To enjoy this life and what it brings
To live your life like a rich king
To let others join us just for fun
Life's for sharing and for fun
Don't threaten someone with a gun
Don't scare them away
Or make them run
Having a life is a pleasure
Do what you want with your life
But be sure!

Thomas Nathan Lamb (11)
Heworth Grange Comprehensive School, Gateshead

I Have A Dream

I have a dream to make the world smile
To achieve something successful, to be a special person
To make people's day with a giggle or two
That's what I'd love to do
To make people feel better
To be an inspiration, and care for everyone dearly.
To change people's emotions with just a smile or a giggle
Or just to be cheerful, I'd love to do this too.

All of this comes from a heart of gold and a part of me too
This is my mum who is as solid as gold
Who is my inspiration and my role model too!

Alisa Amine (12)
Heworth Grange Comprehensive School, Gateshead

42

I Have A Dream

I have a dream of a world that cares for animals but still eats food like chicken, duck and fish.
I have a dream that everyone has a pet even if it is not a cat, a dog or hamster.
People like monkeys, spiders or scorpions.
That people do not hunt tigers and lions and tigers and lions do not attack people
And that you could feed wild animals and they do not attack and act like house pets.

Matthew Thirlwall (13)
Heworth Grange Comprehensive School, Gateshead

Alan Shearer

He grew up on the Tyneside estates
Little did he know he'd be so great.
Now a teen he went to the Toon
Now he's trying to save them goin' doon.

In the name of Alan Shearer
The new Geordie era.
He wears the number nine
Shining all the time.

At the end of his career he hung up his boots
The man was a magpie down to his roots.
St James's Park, his home ground
The Geordie atmosphere spun his head round and round.

The Newcastle fans though he was king
It was only his name they would sing.
One last game away to Villa
If we won he'd sleep well on his pilla.

He doesn't need guns, not ammunition
He is killing them all on his own little mission
One more thing to say, 'Shearer! Shearer!'

Kyle Kane & Jamie Lake (13)
Jarrow School, Jarrow

A Little Bit Longer

He was on Broadway when he was young
A little bit longer
He was bullied for being on Broadway
A little bit longer
His musical talent was discovered at seven
A little bit longer
He brought out his first album at seven
A little bit longer
He made a band with his brothers
A little bit longer
They brought out an album when he was twelve
A little bit longer
Altogether they've brought out four albums
A little bit longer
But when he was fourteen
He was diagnosed with diabetes
He thought it was the end of his world
But Nick Jonas keeps going on
A little bit longer
And he'll be fine.

Laura Taylor(13)
Jarrow School, Jarrow

Your World

Our ozone layer
Is slowly being destroyed
By harmful gases
And other things more.
The future generation
Is now in our hands.
To save the planet
For the precious things in life
Your world, you can help.

Kara Hodgson & Kathryn Smith (13)
Jarrow School, Jarrow

A Single Word

A single word can change the world
No matter how it's said.
If shouted out for all to hear
Or thought within a head.

A single word can change our thoughts
About the world today
It can change the things we think and do
And even what we say.

A single word can change the rules
Of things like political correctness.
But how is it that when some words are said
It doesn't even affect us?

A single word can change it all
If Christian, Muslim or Jew.
No matter your gender or your race
It can change the world for you.

Lucy Charlton (12)
Jarrow School, Jarrow

Angelina Jolie

One minute isn't very long
To act Miss Pong
To save a child
Make it unwild.
One minute really is too short
She owns a port
She is the best
She's not a pest.
And yet it's clearly long enough
To be so tough
To change the world
With her hair curled.

Sarah Wilson (12) Nicola Harkus (13) & Kayleigh Louise Dufour (12)
Jarrow School, Jarrow

45

Rhyme Royal Of Princess Diana

Princess Diana born 1st of July
Helped a lot of people in her short life
She married Prince Charles, their love was so high
Gave birth twice, still a wonderful wife
Though however hard she tried, marriage comes with strife
Charity work she did and came out strong
Though now dead, remembered forever long.

Kelly Whitfield & Fern Davidson (13) & Ashleigh McGeary (12)
Jarrow School, Jarrow

Ian Porterfield

He's a Sunderland hero
'73 FA Cup Final, he scored the only goal
Cos Leeds scored zero
Saved from a future of mining coal
His first club was Raith Rovers
He also managed Chelsea
He'll never have to pick four-leaf clovers.

Daniel Cooper (13)
Jarrow School, Jarrow

I Believe

I believe that whether you're black or white you should be treated the same.
I believe countries should not fight or go to war.
I believe bullying shouldn't ever happen.
Why should people be judged by their appearance?
It doesn't matter what you look like!
I believe people should believe in what they want to
I believe many people in this world can make a change.
I also believe I can make a change!

Louise Maloney (14)
Parklands High School, Liverpool

Changing The World

Imagine a world were people were nice
Imagine a world where people were polite
Imagine a world were people didn't fight

That would be nice, that would be nice.

Imagine a world where people were not judged
By the colour of their skin
But for the character that lies within.
Where children could play and not feel like prey
No matter what time of night or day.

But we live in a culture where fighting is rife
And our lives are filled with pain and strife.

Living today is not easy at all
Keep your eyes open and stay on the ball.

Changing the world would be nice to do
It would be easy apart from a few

Who run with the sheep and play with knives
And end up in jail but, that's their lives.

Imagine changing the world completely
We are capable, you and me.

Ryan Peters (14)
Parklands High School, Liverpool

Changing

Change the poem, change the line,
Change the meaning, change the rhyme.
Change the outcome, change the plan,
Change the mood, change the man.
Change the world!
Can you do it?

Ryan McCaffery (14)
Parklands High School, Liverpool

Changing The World

I have a dream that could change the world
To unite all differences and bring peace to the Earth
There would be no rights and there would be no wrongs
We would all come together like lyrics in a song.

The colour of your skin would not mean a thing
Because in our hearts and our minds
Each and every one of us would be the same
There would be no racism and there would be no fear
Of being judged by our size, our shape or even our hair colour.

Our day would be like our night and our night would be like our day
We would live each moment with grace and joy
And see what heads our way.

I've been told many words of wisdom
That have helped me through my life so far such as:

'Life's too short to be held back
So don't hold grudges and stay on track.'
This is my dream, how I would change the world
It would be a better place with love and care spread around.

Rebecca Taggart (14)
Parklands High School, Liverpool

Why?

Why are there people with guns and knives on the street?
There should be children running around eating sweets.
Why are there bodies always being found?
There should be no war all around.
Why do people drink alcohol and take drugs?
There are too many rapists and too many thugs.
Why don't people get on with each other in life?
Throw away the gun, the drugs and the knife!
Why do people drink and drive?
Do they really want to stay alive?

Jordanne Liggett (14)
Parklands High School, Liverpool

Imagine

Imagine the world full of peace and happiness
Imagine the world without war and tragedy
Imagine the world where nobody was lonely
Imagine the world without bullies
Imagine the world where nobody was on the streets
Imagine the world where nobody treats you badly
Imagine the world where different races didn't matter
Imagine the world without the people who take the Mick out of religion
Imagine the world without crime and wars
Imagine if the people in Africa weren't starving
Imagine if the world wasn't getting polluted
Imagine all the people living under the one sky
Without violence and hate and sadness
Imagine your community uniting with others
It doesn't matter if you're black or white, Jewish or Muslim
It matters about being yourself
Care about others, just do what's right
Try and live a life of peace
And remember imagine . . .

Gary Hill (14)
Parklands High School, Liverpool

Changes To The World

Imagine a world with no wars, guns, fights, people breaking laws.
A world with no violence, just fun, laughter and silence
To teach people that racism is bad, so let them see
We all deserve the right to set each other free.
Helping others from feeling insecure unlike others who are ignorant
and immature
Making a difference in life, a change to the world
Instead of letting others, struggle and strive.
Imagine the world a better place, nobody being judged by the colour of
their face.

Adele McGrath (14)
Parklands High School, Liverpool

49

World Change

We got to start
Making changes
Learn to see people's brothers
Not distant strangers.

All I see are
Racist faces
Misplaced hate
And disgrace to races.

No one should suffer
No one should die
We have to end it
We have to try.

End the violence
End the hate
Make this world
A better place.

Harley David Pendleton (14)
Parklands High School, Liverpool

I Have A Dream

I nspiration

H armony

A ccepting all people

V arieties of people living together

E mpathy

A place with no hatred

D ivisions between races is wrong

R emembering what it used to be like so it won't be like it again

E very person living together with no war

A place in the world for everyone

M en and women working with each other in empathy.

Jonathan Matthew Aindow (13)
Parklands High School, Liverpool

Is It Certain?

Is it certain whether you wake just to hear that noise every morning?
Is it certain that trees do keep us going?
Is it certain that boy really likes you?
Is it certain you'll grow up to be what your dreams clarified?
Is it certain that someone dies in 'EastEnders' tomorrow?
Is it certain a spaceman was born as I wrote 'Certain'?
Is it certain knife is spelt with a K?
Is it certain that the sky is blue?
Is it certain we just can't fly?
Is it certain there is a man or woman?
Is it certain that the Earth is actually round?
Is it certain that we will eventually shake hands with our enemies?
Is it certain we feel there's just no chance?
Is it true people will see their true reflection?
Is it certain we will all be united?
Well then, what is certain?
Will it stop?

Francess Gannon (14)
Parklands High School, Liverpool

What If?

What if
All wars came to an end?
What if
The starving no longer had to starve?
What if
The poor became wealthy?
What if
All races were treated as equals?
What if
You stopped what you were doing
To help someone in need?
Just what if?

Lewis Fleetwood (14)
Parklands High School, Liverpool

I Believe

I believe that a black face should be looked at the same as mine.
I believe that religion should be worshipped and not judged.
I believe that every person, black or white,
Asian or African should be treated as equal and as an individual.
I believe that every voice should be heard and inspired
No matter how little words may seem to mean.
I believe it takes a great deal of courage to stand up to your enemies,
But even more to stand up for your friends.
I believe that Martin Luther King, also Princess Diana made a change.
I believe if they can, I can and if we can, anyone can.
And when that day comes where we can sleep at night with no worry or doubt
Pain or sorrow, that is when we can truly call the world, home.
I believe I can make a difference, can you?

Amie Doyle (14)
Parklands High School, Liverpool

Don't You

Don't you just want to wake up in the morning sometimes
Sometimes without worrying whether you will have a job in the recession?
Don't you just want to wake up in the morning
Knowing that another soldier isn't dying in a war
Losing their life for maybe £200 every few weeks?
Without worrying about global warming
The disease and famine spreading round the world
Walking down the street
Without worrying about the colour of your skin.

One day black and white people
Can live in harmony with one another.
Every person will have their own place and importance in the world
And feel they are special and wanted.

Alan Ramsden (14)
Parklands High School, Liverpool

Imagine

Imagine the world was a better place
Not getting judged by the colour of our face.

Imagine there were no guns or gangs
Young lads stop talking gangster slang.

Imagine there was no racism or bullying
You could be the way you want, just singing.

Imagine there was no one mugging
And there were more people hugging.

Imagine the world a different place
And not getting judged by your race.

Just imagine?

Jade Lamb (14)
Parklands High School, Liverpool

Imagine

Imagine
You could walk round the streets without fear
Without a doubt in your mind
That a gun might be near.

Imagine
You could live in a world with peace and love
And everyone was respected.

Imagine
Everyone worked together
To make the world a better place.
Imagine
One of these people was you.

Shannen Devine (14)
Parklands High School, Liverpool

Just A Dream?

Hot without cold
Just isn't the same.
Winter without wind
Snow or rain?

Summer without sun
It doesn't seem real.
Happy but no sad
Touch but no feel?

A world without war
And no one being mean.
Instead of fighting against each other
Why not just work as one team!

Hannah Fletcher (13)
Parklands High School, Liverpool

Black And White

Black and white, same races, different faces,
Same futures but different colour faces.

There are lots of races but different faces
People are white, black, Asian and lots more
There are lots of races but really I am lying because there's only one race
And that is the human race.
It doesn't matter what colour you are, or where you are from,
You still have the right to stop racism.
Everyone has the right to stop it
Really, there is no point being racist because everyone is the same
Black and white, same race, different face.

Conor McInerney (13)
Parklands High School, Liverpool

The Perfect World

Can you picture a world where race is not an issue
Or where nobody dies on the street?
Can you picture a world where war never happens
Or where poverty is a thing of the past?
Can you picture a world where everyone is equal
Or where money doesn't cause so much trouble?
Can you picture a world where global warming isn't real
Or when everyone is in perfect health?
Can you picture a world where everyone is respected for who they are
Or where drugs are only used to help people?
I can picture this world, can you?

Lauren Farrell (13)
Parklands High School, Liverpool

Racism

There was a girl who was hurt
When she was walking in a pink T-shirt
But she was also in pain
Because people were being so vain
They were being horrible because she was not white
So she started putting up a fight
She had a different speech
But people could teach
She could not relate
So she had to wait
Don't be horrible because we are all different.

Rebecca Houghton (14)
Parklands High School, Liverpool

The World

W onder what the world would be like with no crime
O ld and young can live peacefully and happily
R espect black and white
L ove and peace, people treated exactly the same, poor or with fame
D eath to the people who hate each other
P rayers for different communities combined as one
E vil-minded people may not react
A live, not slavery, treated the same
C rying babies will soon be happy
E nd of hate, black and white will live as one.

Saffron Connor (14)
Parklands High School, Liverpool

Poem

I have a dream, a dream of world peace.
I have a dream that people will treat others as equals.
I have a dream that white, black and foreign can live together in peace.
I have a dream that other aren't treated as slaves.
I have a dream that no one will starve.
I have a dream, what's yours?

Bryan Crabtree (14)
Parklands High School, Liverpool

I Have A Dream, Why?

Why can't everybody be seen as equal?
Why can't more people stand up for what they believe?
Why does it take hurt to make a change?
Why do people fight because they're different?
Why can't the world be a peaceful place?
Why? Why? Why?

Bobby Townson (14)
Parklands High School, Liverpool

Change The World

Every day the world is getting worse
With global warming approaching
Animals, even people are becoming extinct.
The world's resources, we are choking, stop now
And think of a way to save our planet for us, today!

Kayleigh Rogers (13)
Parklands High School, Liverpool

I Have A Dream

I have a dream it's in my sight
To bring the world to a brighter light
To end all wars between every nation
And bring peace and celebration.

I have a dream to help all land
To end cruelty to man we must make a stand
To heal the sick and help the poor
This is only part of my dream, there's much more.

Jamie Richardson (14)
Parklands High School, Liverpool

We Shall Fight

We shall fight against racism
We shall fight against crime
We shall fight against terrorism
We shall fight against prejudice
We shall fight against slavery
We shall fight in every country
In every continent in the world

We shall fight for good over evil.

Adam Laughton (12)
Range High School, Formby

Inspiration

The courage, the bravery,
Of that one soldier,
On the battlefield,
Knowing he could die,
Any,
Second,
now!
Losing everything,
For his countries' rights.
Similar to those,
Who fought for black rights,
But did it peacefully,
'When Rosa sat,
So that Martin could stride,
And Obama ran,
So that our children could fly!'

Teachers inspire,
Their job in life
To educate children
Who wouldn't learn otherwise.
They are dedicated to learning
And pass on knowledge,
That if we didn't have,
We might not survive.
But where would they be
Without writers and musicians
Who give them what they need
To teach us all these
New sights, sounds, even new worlds,
With new thoughts to expand our minds?

More importantly to me,
Where would I be
Without my kind and caring grandad,
Who strives to show me
What I want to see
And helps me find out
What I want to learn?
He is my inspiration!

Matthew Hobbs (12)
Range High School, Formby

Winter's Hidden Treasure

I see a single snowflake
Falling to the ground,
It seems to be a startled bird
Flying up and down.

That single little snowflake
Winter's hidden treasure,
It flutters like a butterfly
Gliding through the heather.

An inspirational snowflake
Unique as you and me,
Whirling and twirling round and round
Just like a silver key.

A snowflake is pure beauty
And not a single noise,
Just like a ballerina
With elegance and poise.

The snowflake is racing,
From the sunny sky,
Faster than a runner
And that is not a lie.

A sparkling little snowflake
Shining like a star,
Yellow in the sunlight
Like a pure gold bar.

Blown onto my fingers
Melting on my hand,
The world is in all snowflakes
And every grain of sand.

I'll cherish that moment
In my head for evermore,
Enjoy it when I want to,
Nature I adore.

Katy Minko (12)
Range High School, Formby

You Decide

Different words,
Have different meanings,
You *decide,*
What you want them to mean.

Fire - destroying homes and snatching lives,
Death - eating away at the ones we love till there's nothing left,
Water - drowning all hope and love, letting hatred rise to
                                        the surface,
Time - ticking away, bringing us ever closer to the brutal sting
                                        of reality,
Smiles - wiped off the faces of children, replaced with the stain of
                                        a tear.

Different words,
Have different meanings,
You *decide,*
What you want them to mean.

Fire - bringing hope and warmth with its precious golden flames,
Death - being fought and conquered - we will never surrender,
Water - rehydrating bodies and coaxing green life,
Time - letting us live every second of our lives to the full,
Smiles - creeping on to everyone's face like a golden whisper.

Different words,
Have different meanings,
You *decide,*
What you want them to mean.
You *decide.*

Lottie Holloway (11)
Range High School, Formby

Hope

A pot of gold over the rainbow,
A ray of sunlight in the dark,
A spot of sunshine in the rain,
A helping hand that's left its mark.

An oasis in the desert,
The northern star in the night,
A flower blooming in your garden,
A death leading to light.

A stronghold in times of hurt,
A friend for you to ring,
A hand for you to hold,
A stage for you to sing.

An oven for you to cook,
A map on a road trip,
A key to open a door,
Some water for you to sip.

A bag for your essentials,
A bookmark for your book,
A pen for you to write,
Some glasses to help you look.

An angel to guide you,
A painting that you made,
A bed for you to sleep in,
A flower that never fades.

Rosie Meehan (11)
Range High School, Formby

Dream Land

I will soar through the air,
With the wind in my hair.
I can fly through the clouds,
So silent - no sounds.

Spread my wings by my side,
There is no need to hide.
No one will find me here,
I can face my greatest fear.

Looking down on the land,
And the river and the sand.
No need to hurry,
I've got nothing to worry.

Looking closely at a dove,
So intricate - I love
To be a bird in the sky,
Higher than high.

I can feel free,
With no one but me.
Just the stars and the sun,
Having so much fun.

But when I see my friends,
My dream land ends,
But only for a while,
A short but steady mile . . .

Laura Tighe (12)
Range High School, Formby

Inspirations

Don't walk, don't run, just fly.
Fly to the inspirations in the sky.
The teachers, the learners,
The friends, the fame.
If you lose faith,
They help bring it back again.
Because of these people who say
That everything will be OK,
Parents, Obama, Rosa Parkes, friends,
They'll keep you strong until the end.
Perseverance, nature, cultures, dreams,
Can inspire you, as crazy as it seems.

Martin Luther King,
Rosa Parkes,
Barack Obama.
They stood their ground or followed their dreams,
And those dreams became reality.
Your parents and friends help you believe,
That anything is possible,
If you just believe you can do it.
If you believe in yourself,
Inspire yourself.
If you believe, inspire and achieve,
Achieve your goals because of those people,
Those people who inspire you!

Hannah Jackson (12)
Range High School, Formby

We Are All Born Free

A midst barbed wire
M y candle flickers
N o freedom for me
E xists in this world
S uffering for my beliefs
T orture and pain
Y earning for home

I long for flight
N o more a prisoner
T o soar up into the clear sky
E very day I long to be
R eunited with my family
N ever caged again
A ll hope seems lost
T hen a miracle
I nto my hands a letter - just a letter
O rdinary people across the world champion my rights
N ow my spirit soars
A midst barbed wire my candle burns brightly
L ighting injustice for the world to see.

We are all born free.

Emily Hobbs (11)
Range High School, Formby

I Believe

I believe,
I believe that one day white people will treat black people
The way they would like to be treated.
I believe,
I believe that one day fortunate people like us
Will take more care of disabled people.
I believe,
I believe that one day parents will stop rows forever
In front of their children.
I believe,
I believe that one day child abuse
Will stop once and for all.
I believe,
I believe that one day charities will have
Over 100,000,000 pounds to spend.

I believe,
I believe the world will be a better place.

Anthony Malpeli (11)
Range High School, Formby

Change

A man once said, 'I have a dream, a dream that all men shall be
Equal and the world could live as one.'
A woman once refused to give up a seat. She was jailed.
A man once said, 'I have a dream.' That man was assassinated.
A man once said, 'Yes we can.' That man was elected president
Of the United States of America.
'This is your victory America.' Barack Obama 44th president of the
USA.
A man once said, 'Free at last! Free at last! Thank God Almighty, we are
free at last!'

History and change all of it and all in the history of blacks.
I have a dream that the world's nations and races will be as one.
You may say I am a dreamer, but I'm not the only one.
This poem is inspired because change will and does happen.

Connor Dolan (12)
Range High School, Formby

My Inspiration

My inspiration
Has been for so many years
Seven books. Brilliant

My inspiration
One author. One great talent
Always my hero

My inspiration
Characters loved by many
Never forgotten

My inspiration
Insight into another world
The J K Rowling.

Beth Mulhall (12)
Range High School, Formby

Inspiration

I n situations of grief and despair, through times of loneliness,

N eed and depression,

S elf belief is powerful, as is the ability to have enough audacity
to aspire to your dreams -

P ursue them until the end.

I n difficult circumstances,

R efusing to feel melancholy, beleaguered,

A nd insignificant is the answer to success;

T herefore we must be courageous,

I n order to live throughout our lives thankfully, joyfully:

O ppression no longer burdening and burning in our souls.

N egativity has no place within our hearts, filled with the
exultant chorusing of pride, freedom, and individuality.

Naomi Adam (11)
Range High School, Formby

I Will

I will stand up for myself and everyone around me,
I will fight for myself and everyone around me,
I will persevere in everything that I do.
As long as you follow your heart
To the path you want to walk down,
One step, two steps, three steps, four . . .
Then you will achieve your dreams
And your dreams will become reality.
I will get what is right for me, for you, for the country.
You could run to the end of the Earth and back,
If you believe in yourself!
Always think big.
You can do it, I can do it, and together it will work.

Janine Cork (11)
Range High School, Formby

Perfect World

P eace on Earth
E quality for all
R ights and justice
F reedom for mankind
E njoyment forever
C reation and sharing
T ruth and honesty

W ell-being and good health
O pportunity and success
R espect and friendship
L ove and kindness
D ays of happiness.

Thomas Hughes (11)
Range High School, Formby

The Animals I Would Like To Work With When I Grow Up

I want to work with:

One dog
Two little cats
A big, green frog
Three tiny rats
A little bunny that wiggles
A hamster that will go
Even if it's in the snow
I think I'll name one Sue
I also want a robin
A tiger named Tig
But he must have a cabin
So I might want a pig
That's which animals I want to work with when I grow up
Then again, I might just print them on a cup.

Samantha Rhodes (11)
St Julie's Catholic High School, Liverpool

68

Untitled

A slap, a punch, just like every day,
'Give me all your money!' they would say.
At first it all just passed me by,
But one day she hit me and I broke down and cried.
I was being bullied,
They were wrecking my self-esteem.

It got worse and worse,
They'd steal everything, right to my purse.
If they entered a room,
I had to leave,
I was being bullied,
They'd wrecked my self-esteem.

I wondered why they'd chosen me?
I just didn't understand, I couldn't see.
I thought I needed to hit or tell them back,
Maybe just a very small slap.
But how? She'd tell, even though
I was being bullied and
They'd destroyed my self-esteem.

But then I thought and thought,
And I knew exactly what I had to do.
There would be no more crying,
In the corner of the yard.
I would tell a teacher,
That would sort it out.

And I was right,
It did
And I got my confidence back.
I made friends and they made foes,
I knew no one was completely alone.

Demi Brant (12)
St Julie's Catholic High School, Liverpool

I Have A Dream, A Dream To Believe!

When life gets tough and the tunnel is long
And it seems there's no light,
When dreams seem lost, don't ever give up the fight.
When you think your life doesn't mean a thing,
You must realise we all have gifts.
Look inside, find those things you could have missed.
I have a dream, a dream to believe.
I believe that the angels said to look inside my heart
And hear the song it sings.
All things are possible if you just believe.
We all have the courage, strength and power
To change our lives.
We are all born with greatness inside.
Don't let your fears or tears hold you back from dreams.
Never ever feel like you have to hide.
I have a dream, a dream to believe.
I'll stretch my arms and reach for the stars.
I'll find my shining light.
All things are possible if you just believe.
Don't ever give up on dreams.
Don't ever forget who you are.
Always know wherever you go,
Someday you'll find that shining star.
I have a dream, a dream to believe.
I will survive and grow, this much I know,
For God has told me so.
All things are possible if you just believe.

Chelsea Parkes (12)
St Julie's Catholic High School, Liverpool

My Hero

My mum is my hero,
She's always there for me,
She's never let me down before,
She gave me life you see.

My mum is my hero,
I know she really cares,
She sits me up upon her knee
And runs her fingers through my hair.

My mum is my hero,
I know she loves me a lot,
If I go to do something dangerous,
She'll say, 'Oh no you're not!'

My mum is my hero,
She wipes my tears away,
I always know I can count on her,
And now I'm here to say:

My mum is my hero,
I really love her so,
And Mum, if you can read this,
I just want you to know:

Mum, you are my hero,
You make my world so bright,
And as long as you are near me,
I know I'll be alright.

Ashleigh Collings (12)
St Julie's Catholic High School, Liverpool

Survivor

Stay tough, I know how you feel,
You've got to stay strong; is that a deal?
What's a bully? They have no idea,
They sit back and watch people scared and in fear.
Have hope when there's none,
They pick on me, why?
They're selfish, twisted and sly,
H&M, Next, Juicy, Paul's Boutique,
Black, white, glasses, geek.
Stay strong when you're down,
Keep a smile, not a frown.
'Ignore them,' the teachers say,
So you once again walk away.
You're surrounded by the crew on the floor,
They will go, honestly? For sure.
See, I've been in the same position too,
You're scared, frightened, what should I do?
Don't feel alone, tell someone:
Mum, Dad, friend. It will soon be gone!
It won't be easy, it will take a while,
They're mean, nasty, scary, and vile.
Don't worry, there's always hope,
With someone's help you will cope.
This roller coaster I came through,
And I know that you will too!

Chloe Walsh (12)
St Julie's Catholic High School, Liverpool

She Fell In Love

She fell in love;
With the touch of the black and white notes,
And the feel of the strings against the smooth wood,
She fell in love;
With the crisp song of the voice,
And the sweet sound of anything but silence,
She fell in love;
With the way the wave of sound covered her,
And took her away to somewhere new,
She fell in love;
With the intensity of the atmosphere around her,
And the way the wind sounded so sharp and clean,
She fell in love;
With every flinch of a noise,
Beginning to tell her a story of cheerfulness,
She fell in love;
With the colours of the sound surrounding her,
And that she knew she was awake from her sleep,
She fell in love;
With the fact that she was succeeding in being herself,
And trying to make an impact on the world,
She fell in love;
With the way her life turned out to be:
A fairy tale disguised as a musical dream.

Evie Melling (12)
St Julie's Catholic High School, Liverpool

I Have A Hero

My hero is Kellie
She is never smelly
Kellie is my big sis
I always give her a kiss

She comes with me everywhere
We are like a pair
Hand in hand
It is like we rule the land

She is my role model
Right down to my soul
I love her loads
With my whole heart

She always has my back
At Christmas gets me presents in a sack
She plays with me in puddles
When I am sad she gives me cuddles

Through thick and thin
She will always be there for me
Because she is my big sis
I love her to bits, kiss, kiss, kiss.

Rebecca McKay (12)
St Julie's Catholic High School, Liverpool

My Hero

My hero is my grandad because he is always there
For me wherever I go. I love him so much, he is lovely to me
And always thinks about me.
When he sits down next to me, he makes me feel
Happy and cheerful.
When my grandad gives me a hug, I feel great because
I don't see him that often.
My hero is my grandad!

Cathy Parsons (12)
St Julie's Catholic High School, Liverpool

Growing Up

Sometimes I wonder what I'll be when I grow up,
I could be a dancer, singer, or play a musical instrument.
Drive a truck, help old people, or anything I want.
When I asked my friends,
'What do you want to be?'
They said:
A dancer with shiny shoes,
Work as a vet,
Be a pilot,
Air hostess,
A movie star,
And own a coffee bar!
Then I remember, I can be anything I want.

So I pick up my pen
And begin to write.
At the end of the lesson,
I hand in my work
And my teacher says, 'Very good.'
Then a bright spark flicks through my brain
And I suddenly know what I want to be -
A writer!

Kenya-Louise Kilgallon (11)
St Julie's Catholic High School, Liverpool

Dreams

So if you're an ordinary girl,
Who wishes for a flashy world,
You want to sing, dance or act.

So you want to have fame,
But it's not all a game,
Your grades and work have impact.

Abbie Warren (12)
St Julie's Catholic High School, Liverpool

It Can Happen If We All Come Together

Imagine if we stopped all war,
Then perhaps we could restore
All of the peace and happiness in the world.
Looking back on all of those years,
Full of sadness and lots of tears,
Never had I thought we'd see the day,
When we give up on guns
And just put them out of our way.
A good example is the Twin Towers,
They knocked them down to show they had power.
Loading up with ammunition,
Children aged seven should not be going on a combat mission.
I am one of the many who wish it would stop;
Everyone around us is getting shot.
It's not fair and it's not right,
All of our friends and family going out to fight.
Death and hatred is what it's all about,
So listen to me and hear me out:
Please stop the hatred,
Stop the death,
Why can't we all just be friends?

Sophie O'Hanlon (12)
St Julie's Catholic High School, Liverpool

My Hero

My hero is my mum because she will always be there for me
And she always makes me laugh
I love her to bits
The thing about my mum is that she will never leave me
She will always be there for me for the rest of my life
That's why she is my hero.

Sophie Moore (12)
St Julie's Catholic High School, Liverpool

The Bullies

As I make my way to school each day
To see the girls who break my heart,
I wish I could tell those bullies
'Can you be kind and not so cruel?'

It starts and lasts all day,
I wish they would just go away.
I think to myself, *what have I done?*
I feel so down and depressed.

I hide it away every day;
I don't know what to say to make them go away.
I feel so alone, like a bird that cannot fly,
I feel like the whole world is on top of me.

One thing is for sure:
Never allow anyone to bring you down.
In your mind think happy thoughts,
To make you stronger and hold your head up high.
Never keep silent, and remember,
Bullies are cowards,
One day they will feel the pain they caused you.

Lauren Burgess (13)
St Julie's Catholic High School, Liverpool

Those Three Girls

Here I am again, sitting on the floor with my hurting wounds,
I feel the taste of salt in my mouth and it feels sour and bitter.
My eyes squinting, but I can still see those girls just standing there laughing,
I feel the taste of salt in my mouth and it feels sour and bitter.
I try to get up, this time I can't,
I think they have hit me more this time.
I feel the taste of salt in my mouth and it feels sour and bitter.
I say to myself, keep strong and go and talk to the teacher.
The teachers never believe me and just say, 'Stop lying.'
I walk off with those girls smirking at me.
I feel the taste of salt in my mouth and it feels sour and bitter.
I think, why is it just me and no one else?
My mum says it's because they're jealous but I don't think they are.
I feel the taste of salt in my mouth and it feels sour and bitter.
Why is there only one of me and three of them?
It's just not fair.
I feel the taste of salt in my mouth and it feels sour and bitter.
I just want them to stop
And think of them getting bullied . . .
Just like me.

Natasha Woods (12)
St Julie's Catholic High School, Liverpool

Bullying

As I wake up for school each day,
I dread the day ahead,
Thinking what those girls will say to me,
Oh, how I wish I could stay in bed.
I approach the gates;
Take a small step at a time,
Hoping they will be off ill each day,
But there are so many of them
And so few of me.
Can't they see how they make me feel?
So alone in the world?
With no one to tell,
My life was hell facing them all alone.
But then one day I filled with rage
And told them all to leave me alone.
So from that day on I have a dream
If you too are being bullied,
You can tell someone
And have the courage to stand up to them:
Remember, you are not alone.

Amy Dawson (12)
St Julie's Catholic High School, Liverpool

I Have A Dream

I have a dream
Of a peaceful world:
No war,
No fights,
No crime.
I know this may never happen,
At least not in time.

I have a dream
Of a happy world:
No prejudice,
No racism,
No bullies.
I know this may never happen,
At least not with ease.

I know this poem won't change much,
But they're the things I dream
And I think that's what everyone wants,
Even though that's not how it seems.

Sophie Maysmor (13)
St Julie's Catholic High School, Liverpool

My Family

My family, what's there to say?
Except that we're a great big bunch!

We would be here day and night,
If I mentioned everyone's name,
So we would get very bored
And that would be a shame!

We live all over the UK,
Here, near and far,
But that doesn't stop us,
Being who we are!

Natalie Kirby (12)
St Julie's Catholic High School, Liverpool

My Hero Came Today!

My hero came today,
Not a big, strong man,
He helps people across the road,
Peacemaker: I call him that.

No bullies at schools,
No one leaving out friends,
Everyone is friends in this world.

My heart filled with
Gladness and happiness
Knowing someone is helping
The world.

Now he's left here,
Moved on somewhere
Much bigger,
Maybe, maybe he
Might end
Poverty and war!

Ellie Jeffrey (12)
St Julie's Catholic High School, Liverpool

Peer Pressure

I saw them smoking and drinking at night,
I didn't know whether to join them or turn out the light,
I tried to ignore them,
I tried to walk away,
But they seemed so friendly until this day.

Now I am in prison,
I got really drunk one day,
I attacked a police officer
And got taken away.
Now I regret giving in to temptation that day,
I wish I had ignored them and turned away.

Olivia Welsh (11)
St Julie's Catholic High School, Liverpool

I Stood Up To A Bully Today

She used to slap me, sometimes punch,
She used to wait for me at lunch,
'Give me your dinner money,' she would say,
And I would do so every day.
I would sit alone at lunch and break
And no friends did I make.

I would meet her sometimes on my way to school,
She would always manage to make me look a fool,
By teasing, laughing and making fun you see,
No one could imagine how difficult it was to be me.

This went on for three months, maybe four,
Until I decided I wasn't going to take any more.
I stood my ground and met her by the school gate,
I asked her to explain why she showed so much hate.

I told her that the bullying I could no longer bear,
She told me she was only doing it
Because it used to happen to her.

Niamh Fowler (12)
St Julie's Catholic High School, Liverpool

The School Bully

I stood up to Sarah today
Now she looks at me in a different way.
She used to be mean and take my lunch,
Once she even tried to throw a punch!
But then my friend told me to tell my dad,
And then I wouldn't be so sad.
So I did, I took her advice,
Then Mrs Brown made Sarah be kind and nice.
It seems very strange, but now we're friends,
Yep, best friends forever,
Till the very, very end.

Lauren Shillcock (11)
St Julie's Catholic High School, Liverpool

A Little Poem About Me

I like to go trampolining with my friends
And visit my grandad's
But one day I would like to visit Florida
I love to care for animals, especially my cat
I'm a bit scared of spiders and wasps
My favourite colour is blue
It makes me think of the sky and sea
My favourite subject is DT
Why? Because it's fun and exciting
I'm good at science
I wish I was good at maths even though I hate it!
My school friends are Sarah, Sami, Alex and Rachel
(But I have many more)
We never argue and we have a lot in common
Sometimes I dream about weird things I can't explain!
In the future I'd like to be a vet
If I ruled the world I'd give everyone a pet
(Well, if they wanted one)!

Hannah Green (12)
St Julie's Catholic High School, Liverpool

Growing Up

Giving up silly songs
Rage and anger comes along
Obviously, everything's new
Wishes and dreams that couldn't come true
Imagining goes out the door
No more imaginary wars
Growing up can be so tough
Unless you find a friend it can be quite rough
Past and present can be so different
Wow! I wish I was still in primary!

Rosie King (12)
St Julie's Catholic High School, Liverpool

Bullying

Please stop bullying me,
It hurts so much,
My arm where you bruised
Is so sore to touch.

They pull my hair,
They drag me round everywhere,
I swear, I swear,
I will tell Sir.

I wish they'd go away,
I walk round with fear every day,
I try to obey,
Everything they say.

I wish they'd disappear,
Because every time they're here,
I stand there,
Frozen with fear!

Phoebe Wakefield (12)
St Julie's Catholic High School, Liverpool

Dear Prime Minister

Why haven't you made any changes?
You promised once the job was yours
Everything would be different
You haven't done anything yet though
There are still people without homes
And people without food
I thought they'd be the first things you'd change
There's not enough time
People are dying, when you're not even trying
To save them
You have the power to
And I don't know why you won't.

Gabrielle Gorst (13)
St Julie's Catholic High School, Liverpool

Life Is A Challenge

Life is a challenge,
But you must never give up.
Follow your dreams
Though it may be tough.

With help by your side
You're sure to survive.
You'll find a way
Whatever they say.

If you stick with it
Your effort will show bit by bit.
At the end of the tunnel there will be a light
As long as you have put up a fight.

So follow your dreams
Though it may be tough.
Yes, life is a challenge
But you must never give up.

Lily Currie (12)
St Julie's Catholic High School, Liverpool

My Hero

My mum is my hero, I love her so much
We always spend time together
Loved and tucked up
We spend a lot of time together
And I hope that this lasts always and forever
We have our chats
And our really *big* laughs
Sunshine flowers, glorious hours
Spread quickly away
But our friendship will never fade away
Mum, you are my hero
Don't ever go away!

Eve McHale (11)
St Julie's Catholic High School, Liverpool

My Hero

My hero is someone special,
Who never says no,
They hug the world
And never let go.

My hero saves the world,
They won't let you down,
They smile and smile
And won't give a frown.

They are my idol,
My wannabe,
I love the way they look,
Just at me!

I still love them,
Through the bad and the new,
They are something special,
My hero is you.

Shannon Murphy (12)
St Julie's Catholic High School, Liverpool

My Hero

Oh Mum, oh Mum,
She makes me smile,
I want her to walk me down the aisle.
She lights up the room when she comes in,
And she would never sin.
I love her to bits,
Even if she had zits.
She is so great,
And will always be my best mate.
I love you Mum!

Kerri Caskie (11)
St Julie's Catholic High School, Liverpool

My Dream

I had a lifelong dream,
Since the age of six,
To be the best singer ever
And to make it to the Brits!

To be a solo artist,
Or even in a band,
To have a hit single,
To be the best in the land!

The things I could do are,
Pop, dance or R&B,
I don't know yet,
But we shall soon see!

And now with me,
At the age of eighteen,
I'm living my life,
Like a fantastic dream!

Emma Funcks (13)
St Julie's Catholic High School, Liverpool

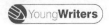

A Dream

A dream I've had,
It's very sad,
I lost everything,
My family, my friends, they all disappeared,
I just didn't have a clue,
Then a voice said to me,
'No family, no friends, just you!'
I didn't know what to do or where to go,
Should I run to the closest thing,
Or stay by myself,
I was so confused,
Then I started to think
And I realised,
If I just opened my eyes,
I'd be home,
Safe and sound,
Back with my mum, family and friends!

Samantha Roberts (12)
St Julie's Catholic High School, Liverpool

My Hero

I love my nan,
As much as our Dan.
I know she will always be there for me!
I love to see her smile,
Even though I haven't seen her for a while.
I'd love her to bits,
Even if she had nits!
Her happy smile and friendly face,
Makes the world a better place.
I remember when I was little,
She had a cat called Tiddle
Who was black and white,
Though she'd never bite!
When she switches off the light,
I won't get a fright
Because I know she
Will always be there for me.

Ceri Moorcroft (11)
St Julie's Catholic High School, Liverpool

Big

I am a little bug
A little bug with a big dream
My dream is to stand up to the big kids
The big kids who step all over my family
My dream is to feel big for once; to feel invincible
To feel as if no one can stop me
I want to do what big people do
To go where big people go
To sleep when big people sleep
To eat what big people eat
And to dream what big people dream
But for now I am me
I will believe whatever I believe
No matter how big or small
Or weak or strong you are
Just say to yourself
I believe.

Janice Musimwa (12)
St Julie's Catholic High School, Liverpool

The Fan

(In loving memory of Patrick Thompson, son, brother and uncle. Rest in peace.)

Cheering away, he began
Smiling at friends; the biggest fan.
He loved it so much.
The hate in his game was as unlikely as a teardrop
In the blinding sun.
Fighting for what he loved most,
People stomped and crushed,
The innocent were gone
But stay forever, in our thoughts.
His inspiration overwhelms my mind.
So much to leave behind:
A family, country and Liverpool FC.
Peace was forgotten for those with no hope,
The possibility of life was ending rapidly in mid-air.
The man, my inspiration: the fan.

Elle Kearney (12)
St Julie's Catholic High School, Liverpool

My Family

When I'm growing up my family are around me,
And when I'm even older I'm sure they still will be.

My mum is on my left, my dad is on my right,
They will always protect me with all of their might.

There are many other members of my family too,
There soon will be another who is brand new.

I am an only child, but only for a while,
I can't wait to see my new baby brother and his lovely smile.

There's going to be a big age difference, twelve years to be exact,
But a brother in my family is exactly what we've lacked.

I'll never be alone again!

Megan Jones (12)
St Julie's Catholic High School, Liverpool

I'll Be There

If something goes wrong in life,
Don't blame yourself
If you are sad or lonely or upset
I'll be there.

If you try to do something, but fail,
Don't stop, you can do it
You just have to believe
I'll be there to help.

I'll be there if you
Need a shoulder to cry on
Or just someone to talk to
I'll always be there.

If you need help with anything
Just ask
I'll be there 24/7.

Emily Kilkelly (12)
St Julie's Catholic High School, Liverpool

My Dream

I had a dream one day that everything had gone away
I didn't have a thing at all, I felt that I was very small.
My friends and family didn't care, all they did was sit and stare.
I had no food, I had no drink,
I had no paper, I had no ink.
So I knew I had to sit and think.
I always waste, I never use,
I suddenly got so confused.
I had taken everything for granted,
So when I woke up the next day,
I had to shout a huge hooray!
Now I never waste, I always use,
And now I'm not so confused.

Jessica Cahill (12)
St Julie's Catholic High School, Liverpool

Say No To Smoking

Last night I had a little dream,
When I woke, I thought it was true.
I was with St Julie's Year 9s,
We were smoking in the loo.

At first I tried to walk away,
But took their advice,
'Come on, just one puff will do,
it's really, really nice.'

I wish I'd listened to my parents,
'Don't smoke, it's not the way.'
Maybe if I'd trusted them,
I'd be in school today.

My advice to anybody, either young or old,
Smoking is distasteful,
So do as you are told.

Kellie Carbery (12)
St Julie's Catholic High School, Liverpool

My Family

This poem is about my family who love and care
And one thing's for sure, they are always there
I have two brothers who are so funny
They can make you laugh until you get a sore tummy
I have three sisters who are so cool
They cheer me up after a bad day at school
My mum and dad are the best
They can help me when I'm down
I think they deserve a crown
I love my family with all my heart
That's why we're never apart
That's the poem about my family who love and care
But one thing's for sure, they are always there.

Olivia Symes (12)
St Julie's Catholic High School, Liverpool

Bullied

A slap, a punch, a kick
Or even a flick
I watch as they laugh so hard
I wish it could be barred.
I don't want to go to school
In case they hit me like a fool
I wish I could fit in
And not be treated like rubbish in a bin.
I wish I could get rid of these fears
So I didn't have any more tears
I wish I could have a better life
And not get threatened by a knife.
Tonight I got hurt
But nobody cared
Not even my mum
She never even heard.

Elle Jones (12)
St Julie's Catholic High School, Liverpool

My Hero

My dad,
He makes me smile every once in a while,
He laughs and jokes,
He's one of my folks,
He helps me with my aims,
But still likes to play games,
When I feel down,
He always turns it around,
And makes my frown turn upside down,
He is so great,
He is like my best mate,
I love him to bits,
And he makes me have laughing fits.

Sophie Robinson (11)
St Julie's Catholic High School, Liverpool

Chance To Dream

Some say it is useless,
And can never reach their goal.
This will make you believe
That your life will never be whole.
Ignore them and reach out
To the dream you've always cared about.
Careless people will say,
That your dream is like the Earth with no sky.
This means they believe in living,
With no shine up high.
The shine that is shining,
Is the door to your dreams.
Always reach for it, no matter how hard it seems.
No one else is around, but there is a key in front of you.
As soon as you take it,
Everything will come true.

Natasha Robinson (12)
St Julie's Catholic High School, Liverpool

Listen To Me, Bully

Bully, bully, bully
That's what you are
Don't you realise you're making a scar

Only losers give hits and bruises
You don't understand this is the fear of his life
For all you know he may pick up a knife
And end his fear
Your death is near

So maybe you should stop
Rise to the top
And be a better man
And make bullying banned.

Ellie Cleghorn (13)
St Julie's Catholic High School, Liverpool

First Day At School

Don't be afraid, it's not that scary,
'Now let's all pray to Mother Mary.'
It's not that big
But it's not that small,
We all have to walk
Slowly down the hall.

There are lots of floors
And many doors,
There are no lockers
To hold our stuff,
Many things are very tough.

Too many books and
Bags to handle,
But pupils look after
Things and do not vandal.

Victoria Hodnett (12)
St Julie's Catholic High School, Liverpool

Life Is Full Of Challenges

Life is full of challenges,
So many different things.
People, school, work, money
And many, many more!

Life is full of challenges,
They make us who we are.
Everyone goes through them,
Who, what, where, when?
Nobody knows when they're going to happen.

So remember:
Don't think you're any different!
Life is full of challenges,
But you can get through them!

Andrea Dunne (12)
St Julie's Catholic High School, Liverpool

96

Bullies Of The World!

Their voices are loud
Their presence is eerie
They try their best to be scary.

They push and shout their way around
Taking people's things,
Pushing them to the ground.

They live their lives
Pursuing the weak
But all they have is a yellow streak.

Deep down they know they're wrong
When you stand up for yourself
You will be strong.

Intimidation, degradation,
They are found in every nation.

Jenna Smith (12)
St Julie's Catholic High School, Liverpool

My Hero

She looks at me with her smiling face,
Nothing seems out of place,
The sun is shining, the wind is at bay,
Looking around the perfect day . . .
With my hero, my star - my nan,
She will help me in any way she can.
Just to see me smile,
Every once in a while.
Her heart is as big as the world;
She's my idol and I'm her girl.
When she talks about death I can't help but cry,
It hurts too much to think of saying goodbye
And with this feeling comes the fear,
To imagine my life without her here.

Elle Barton (12)
St Julie's Catholic High School, Liverpool

My New York Dream

I have a big, imaginary dream,
That I think about every single night,
To go to a place I have never been,
To see from a height, an amazing sight!

This lovely place is called New York city,
Or the Big Apple as some people say.
Landmarks, like the Statue of Liberty,
My biggest dream, to live here some day!

So every night when I sleep in my bed,
I lie down, close my eyes and have my dream,
Smile to myself as I think in my head,
To go to that place where I've never been!

New York, New York, what a lovely city,
Shame I don't live there now, what a pity!

Faye Fearon (12)
St Julie's Catholic High School, Liverpool

Say No To Drugs

S ome people think they're hard taking drugs
A ll they are doing is wasting their life
Y our friends may take them but you shouldn't

N o point in trying to be cool
O ther people may think you're a wimp, at least you won't be
    in jail soon enough

T ry joining a group so you know how it's wrong
O bsession becomes your life

D rugs are wrong and you know it's true
R eally you need help if you start
U gly and apart from your family
G ive up: there's no point in starting
S ave your life before you die suddenly.

Jess Carroll (11)
St Julie's Catholic High School, Liverpool

98

My Nan

My hero is my nan,
She hates getting called 'Gran'
I love her so much
Even though she speaks Dutch.
I hope she's always there,
I hope she'll always care,
My nan, she's the best,
Better than all the rest!
My nan, I love you,
I hope you love me too,
She's the best at everything,
Bingo and cleaning,
That's why her house is always gleaming!
I hope you never change,
Because you're great the way you are!

Amie Ambrose (12)
St Julie's Catholic High School, Liverpool

I Have A Dream

I have a dream to invent something new.
Yesterday, I invented a brand new scooter,
It was pink and blue with a loud hooter.
My mum and dad were proud,
My sister thought I was mad.
It was fast and furious,
Which got children curious.
'Should I buy one? Should I buy one?'
It was big and bold, which stood out from the crowd.
Zip, zip, zip, it went, winning the race - very proud.
It won a medal and trophy,
Which then got the crowd saying, 'Whoo hoo.'
It went back to the factory where more got made,
Now my scooter is the new craze!

Katie O'Malley (12)
St Julie's Catholic High School, Liverpool

It's Because The World Changes

Poor old me aged thirteen
But boy I was keen
I really wanted to be a singer
But I really was a minger
If you think you're the same
Come on, you're not to blame
Hold your head way up high
Listen to me, you don't want to lie
Liars get nowhere, apart from living in a bin
If you have an ambition
There's no competition
If you want all your fans screaming your name
And have loads of fame
Follow your dream
And be in a team.

Katie Brown (13)
St Julie's Catholic High School, Liverpool

My Hero

My hero is my mum
She's not stupid, she's not dumb
She stands by me when things are rough
She stands by me, she is tough
We have been through everything together
Even in the stormy weather
She is my rock, she is my stone
She is there when I have a moan
When I am cold she keeps me warm
She is my rose between two thorns
My mum is a glowing sun
Yes, a glowing sun, that's my mum
She hugs me in the day and night
My mum is my shining light.

Emma Garvey (12)
St Julie's Catholic High School, Liverpool

100

I Have A Dream

I have a dream, as you can see
My dream is to write poetry
And now you see.
Take a look
My dream is inside a book!
This poem might be big
It might be small
But this poem has it all.
Follow your dream
Follow it today
There is no right or wrong way.
But one more thing I want you to know
Well before you go -
Yes, you!
You helped my dream come true.

Alex Rhodes (11)
St Julie's Catholic High School, Liverpool

My Family

They tuck me in bed at night and feed me
They make me happy when I am upset
They have helped me since I was a baby
I know that I can trust them, they are not a threat
Without them I am nothing, just sadness
They are the exit of a scary ride
They have always been goodness, not badness
And in the past I know they've never lied
They are my family, the ones I love
They have always been working very hard
They are angels sent from Heaven above
They have been protecting me like a guard
I will mark them one thousand out of ten
I just cannot picture love without them.

Sophie Larsen (11)
St Julie's Catholic High School, Liverpool

My Hero

My hero always comes to save the day
And stops to see if I am OK
My hero is always on my mind
Because she can be very kind

My hero makes me smile when I am down
By acting like a very silly clown
My hero's name is Liz
She may not seem tough, but she is

My hero is the best
She is better than all the rest
My hero is only round the bend
My love for her will never end.

Leah MacFetters (12)
St Julie's Catholic High School, Liverpool

My Dream

I want to be a gymnast,
One who flies all over the beam.
I want to be a gymnast,
That is my ultimate dream.

I will work so hard,
I will train all day,
Flip all around the floor,
That is the perfect way.

I want to be a gymnast,
One who goes on bars,
I want to be a gymnast,
One that flies as high as Mars.

Kate Turner (12)
St Julie's Catholic High School, Liverpool

I Had A Dream

I had a dream:
I wanted to do well,
To be successful and proud of myself.

I let myself down, always fretting and frown.
I let myself go
But little did I know.

Once you leave school,
Life's not that cool.
There's a big, wide world out there
And sometimes I get scared.
Do well in your GCSEs
And life will come at you with ease.

Amy McKinstry (13)
St Julie's Catholic High School, Liverpool

Unbalanced

Every time I pass a street and see discrimination,
I think of all the inequality in this confusing nation.
On the streets where cars race by
And no one gives a care,
To what goes on outside their car, not even in the air.

For what they do not know, they have no idea,
How people suffer with no money,
Others waste on drugs and beer.
If they could give that money to those who suffer in great pain,
This world would be a better place, but isn't it insane?

Half the world dying of hunger, half of obesity,
So if in those cars people stopped and thought in that busy city,
If in this economic crisis everything was shared out equally,
The world would be improved for them, you and even me.
It would put all of our minds at rest for those people trapped in pain,
For the whole society as a world, it would be a massive gain.

Joanne Kenny (13)
Upton Hall School, Wirral

103

Dream

A little
Dream
Just a hope
A fantasy
Little or big a
Dream is a dream and a hope is a hope
No one can destroy hopes and dreams
Can you
Stop
You
Dreaming
Just
Dream
A
Little
Tiny
Dream.

Elena-Mae Rosewell (12)
Upton Hall School, Wirral

I Wish

I wish that my love could be the world I live in,
The most beautiful garden of Eden.
I wish that the young children of the world
Could no longer live in poverty.
I wish that the people that do more, get more.
I wish that in the silence, someone could stand out.
I wish that a smile could be passed on throughout the world.
I wish that poor people's dreams could come true.
I wish that if you read a book,
The memories would stay in your head forever.
I wish that my best friends would forget me, never.

Lara O'Dowd (12)
Upton Hall School, Wirral

My Dream To Be Happy

When a dove soars, I know it's a dream
When I see a rainbow shine,
I dream that I live a happy life,
Now that seems unreal
To have a family and a happy life.

The road is stretched out before me,
My life's journey is set.
I dream I wake up and see,
The pot of gold waiting to be met.

The sky is clearing, I am free,
To soar just like that dove,
I have found that key, up high above.
I am free, to be me,
My happy family.
Everything is what it seems.

Olivia Sinclair (12)
Upton Hall School, Wirral

I Dare

I dare to know the future,
I dare to change the world,
Because that's what we need to see.
I dare to change the world,
Because there is so much hatred and greed.
Is there any need?
I dare to find courage in me.
I dare, don't you see?
I dare to change the world,
No war, no fighting.
I dare to take a chance.
I dare to stand out.
I dare, do you?

Jennifer McCurdy (12)
Upton Hall School, Wirral

Just To Show I Care So Much

I want to paint and live somewhere far away,
And bring a dog by the name of Oscar,
I would sit under the sun to paint every ray,
Just to show I care so much.

My dedication is like a road going on forever,
I would walk my dog down that long, great road,
Or drift away like a feather,
Just to show I care so much.

But when I finally get discovered,
What if I fall? I always think,
I hope that I will be recovered,
Just to show I care so much.

I'll hold Oscar close through the nights,
To shield us from any terrible frights.

Esmée Finlay (12)
Upton Hall School, Wirral

Sweets

When all the love hearts are gone
And the jelly babies start crying,
When all the jelly snakes have slithered away
Because the milk from the chewy milk bottles is gone,
When all the Skittles have been knocked down
And all the candyfloss has been squashed,
When all the Curly Wurlys have melted
And the last lollipop popped,
When all the fizzy apples are picked
And the popcorn starts popping,
Then I'll feel sick and my teeth
Will be full of fillings.

Yes, I have a dream
That sweets will be good for me!

Betty Wilson (12)
Upton Hall School, Wirral

106

My Dream Life

I have a dream which I frequently see,
I am standing, holding, nursing a cat.
It has been cured from a fatal disease,
So it runs out the door and that is that.

Next, I am standing outside a large house,
It is homely, cosy and mine for now.
Inside here, there isn't the smallest mouse.
This is my home; I can hear you say wow.

Four smiling people live happily there,
Me, of course, and my handsome husband too.
Plus a boy and a girl with long, blonde hair.
I love this life, I really truly do.

But still, no matter how much it will seem,
That wonderful life was only a dream.

Rachel Fitchett (13)
Upton Hall School, Wirral

Wishes

Wishes are a fantasy
You think about them all the time
Wishes are for you and me
I know a wish of mine.

I wish that High Street clothes would come at low prices.
I wish that animals could talk.
I wish that there was a pot of gold at the end of a rainbow.
I wish that models could be all shapes and sizes.
I wish that when I'm older I could become an actress.
I wish that I could go to New York.
I wish that computers wouldn't get viruses.
I wish that my mum could win the lottery.
I wish that my moneybox had hundreds of pounds in it.
I wish that dreams would come true.

Amy McCann (12)
Upton Hall School, Wirral

Music Within Me

When I say *singer*, people think of fame
But I think of emotions, lyrics and passion
When I say fame, people think game
Magazines, celebrities, TV and the latest fashion.

When I utter *music awards*, people say Katy Perry and Britney Spears
Hollywood, cameras and a red carpet dress
But I think joy, glamour and tears
And a nation they managed to impress.

When people say *charts*, they think who's number one?
I think of the many songs that touched my heart
And a race that chart toppers have won.

When I say *piano*, people think notes like Es and Cs
But I think of the legends like Stevie Wonder
And Alicia Keys.

Abela Kabyemela (13)
Upton Hall School, Wirral

I Have A Dream

I dream that summer lasts all year long
I dream that daffodils grow instead of weeds
I dream that chocolate grows on trees
I dream that animals can talk
I dream that reading a book brings it to life
I dream that uniform doesn't exist
I dream that tears are laughter
I dream that superheroes aren't only in comics
I dream that flying is easy
I dream that fairies wash the dishes
I dream that there is no such thing as sickness
I dream that hate is the new love
I dream that the Queen lives in Upton
I dream that I will live forever.

Olivia Parrington (12)
Upton Hall School, Wirral

I Hope!

I hope that natural becomes the new fake,
I hope that African music takes over hip-hop,
I hope that one day people will give a dog a home,
I hope that fossil fuels become renewable,
I hope that Martin Luther King comes back to life,
I hope that shopping becomes a sport
And I hope that the library is the cool new hangout.
I hope that men care about women for who they are
And not what they look like!
I also hope no one knows how to use a bomb.
I hope that the top I really wanted is reduced to £2,
I hope that the Internet is one of the safest places to be,
I hope that the police are like they were in the 1970s,
I hope that people want happiness rather than fame,
I hope you don't put yourself back in the fire again.

Alex McNee (13)
Upton Hall School, Wirral

I Imagine

I imagine a world without war
I imagine an alien is invading Earth
I imagine the government banning school
I imagine ice cream and pizza for dinner
I imagine everyone living their lives to the fullest
I imagine a world without poverty
I imagine everyone always happy
I imagine everyone in history coming back to life
I imagine the sun shining every day
I imagine ice cream never melting
I imagine that no one ever grows old
I imagine that everyone is friends
I imagine all the ill will be cured
I imagine a world without end.

Sian Rogan (12)
Upton Hall School, Wirral

I Imagine

I imagine that aliens will roam the Earth,
I imagine sweets become vegetables,
I imagine that I own my own private island,
I imagine that I could fly a jumbo jet,
I imagine that my brain will be filled with information
At the click of my finger,
I imagine that all teachers have big, blue hair,
I imagine essays write themselves,
I imagine that I can drink hot chocolate till I burst,
I imagine that it would be against the law to go to school,
I imagine that everyone could speak every language,
I imagine that I can watch films with my eyes closed,
I imagine that all children can drive,
I imagine that I own a mansion,
I imagine that all celebrities live in my road.

Mary Beth Lamb (13)
Upton Hall School, Wirral

I Dream

I dream
That flowers would grow wherever you sang
That people could understand each other without words being said
That food would taste however you wanted it to
That people wanted things for others instead of themselves
That daydreams would become real when you fell asleep
That money gave you happiness instead of riches
That when you brought home seashells, you could see the sea
That books could be more precious than any diamond
That home could be your personal world
That at school, children would learn to fly
That diseases were only spread by not eating enough chocolate
That following your heart would be as easy as thinking of dreams
I dream.

Amy Simpson (13)
Upton Hall School, Wirral

My Beliefs

What I believe is that dreams come true
When I look in your eyes.
I believe the future is ours
So why not grab it now?
Change is what I believe in
But will it come in time?
I believe a small essence of truth
Can shape the future when I look at you.
Small actions grow
And change happens when you kiss me.
But do you, my love, believe?
Do you believe in me?
When you are gone
All these beliefs go with you, my dear.

Jennifer Welsh (13)
Upton Hall School, Wirral

I Dream

I dream that one day the world will change
I dream that one person will turn a light off
And help save the world
I dream that one day a light will appear
A glowing, never fading light
Brightening up a person's life
A chance of freedom
I dream that black and white will unite
I dream that differences will be forgotten
I dream that a smile will change the direction of somebody's day
I dream that somebody asks an unheard person's opinion
I dream that one simple action will make a person think a different way
I am dreaming of a future for me and you
I just want these dreams to come true.

Jennifer Derry (12)
Upton Hall School, Wirral

My Many Hopes

I hope I'm a vet when I'm older
I hope animals learn to talk
I hope cures are given out for free
I hope that bills are banished
I hope it's sunny tomorrow
I hope ice lollies are healthy
I hope puppies stay little forever
I hope technology doesn't get more confusing
I hope hot dogs become the new vegetables
I hope I can live in Disney World
I hope I have mash and sausages for tea
I hope footballers get paid realistic wages
I hope emergency services get more credit
I hope my family stay safe forever.

Alison Gallagher (13)
Upton Hall School, Wirral

I Dream

I dream,
There will never be a meteor shower,
Even if it doesn't devour,
Fashion will be extinct,
People's individuality will shine through,
Teddies would talk,
Fish would walk,
Dogs will talk our language,
Homework won't exist,
There will be no more bills to pay,
Money will grow on trees,
Bees and wasps won't sting,
Poor will be the new rich,
I dream.

Sophie Holmes (13)
Upton Hall School, Wirral

Just Believe

I've never thought that a dream could come true,
Or that change could make a difference.
I didn't think my voice would be heard,
My actions seemed to always be the smallest.
Neither did I consider that I could shape my future,
Or that the truth could work magic sometimes.
I just didn't have hope left inside me,
Until I learned how to believe.
Now I see the world so much more freely,
I have found so many possibilities.
Now I do understand that a dream can come true,
If I can do it, of course you can too.
So don't give up, as hard as it may seem,
Because anything can happen when you learn to believe.

Jade Laverick (12)
Upton Hall School, Wirral

Imagine

I believe in dreaming
I believe it's right
I believe it's a gift
Day or night
Imagine a place without looks
No one to laugh at your hair
Imagine a place with total respect
Wouldn't you love to live there?
Imagine a place full of laughter
No one would seem to care
Imagine a place without money
Everyone just shared
Imagine a place full of sun
No one to spoil the fun.

Gabriella Shannon (13)
Upton Hall School, Wirral

I Dare!

I dare to dye my hair pink for school.
I dare to confront people when they make nasty comments.
I dare to try my hardest in school and concentrate a lot more.
I dare not to be anyone but myself.
I dare to express my true feelings.
I dare to do my own thing.
I dare to challenge problems head-on.
I dare to love my enemies.
I dare to stare into the eye of danger.
I dare not to get into a bad mood when things come my way.
I dare to go skiing on a trip when I am older.
I dare to go on the biggest roller coaster in Blackpool.
I dare to cook a hot chilli dinner for my family.

Katie Hughes (13)
Upton Hall School, Wirral

Stranger Things Have Happened

I hope that talents get spotted
I hope that I get a letter from Hogwarts
I hope Coldplay do a free concert
I hope I have a koala bear as a pet
I hope everyone looks and feels indifferent
I hope to start a new trend
I hope I get a free holiday
I hope to become a vampire
I hope for unlimited iced tea
I hope that hope happens.

Sally Waddington (13)
Upton Hall School, Wirral

I Dream

I dream that one day the world will change.
I dream the light will never fade.
I dream people will come together.
I dream the world will be one.
I dream actions will speak louder than words ever could.
I dream there will be a light for all the world to see.
I dream you'll look inside your mind.
I dream you'll be inspired.
I dream you won't stand in a crowd.
Dream, speak out, be loud.

Beth Jones (13)
Upton Hall School, Wirral

A Little Fall Of Rain

I dream that after every rainfall there is a rainbow.
I dream that every blossom blooms.
I dream that karma is real.
I dream that 'home sweet home' is not just a saying.
I dream that books become the new DVDs.
I dream a happy dream.

Sarah Murphy (12)
Upton Hall School, Wirral

I Have A Dream

I have a dream where no man does another man's bidding.
Everyone has a right to free speech, no person is enslaved.
Blood diamonds will be replaced with jewels of a different kind,
Nobody is afraid or threatened,
No wars, just peace.

I have a dream . . .

Laura Atkin (13)
Walbottle Campus Technology College, Newcastle upon Tyne

I Have A Dream . . .

Could you imagine
A world with some hope?
There would be no more abuse,
So that children could cope . . .

I have a hope,
That there really, really should
Be no more starvation,
A kinder world would be good!

A child would aim
To do well in school,
To try and fly high,
Then not be a fool.

I had a thought
There would be no more war,
There would be peace in the world,
Then there's just a few more . . .

A singer would like
To sing in key,
A skier would like
To be able to ski.

An author would dream
To sell lots of copies,
A florist would like
To purvey lots of poppies . . .

I have a plea,
A new, kind age,
No more racism,
Now let's start the change!

I have a dream
For all this to happen,
To fit together
All in a pattern.

Emma Fidler (12)
Walbottle Campus Technology College, Newcastle upon Tyne

I Have A Dream, A Wonderful Dream

I have a dream
Where children are free
War has ended
Where sun shines down on our heart
Where animals can be set free
Starvation has gone, flown away.

In with the future, out with the past
People can believe in what they want
No one will be alone
You can set your feelings free.

Poverty has ended
There are jobs for everyone
Feel secure, feel safe
Crime has gone, flown away.

You can do whatever you want
Racism has gone, flown away
You can feel safe here
No one can ever be tortured again
Money doesn't matter, no one cares
All you need is your family and friends.

The world can be our dream
All we have to do is believe
Pollution has gone, never to be heard again
This is my dream and it can happen.

Everything is possible
If only we believe
Oh, we can make this reality
All we have to do is believe.

Kim Kime (12)
Walbottle Campus Technology College, Newcastle upon Tyne

I Have A Dream

I have a dream that everyone can be nice to each other
No matter what.

I have a dream that everyone who has been kind, caring and helpful
Should have their dreams come true.

I have a dream that bullying will stop because bullies are people
Who don't like themselves, so pick on other people's insecurities.

I have a dream that no one should give up on their dreams
And will fulfil their potential.

I have a dream that anyone who makes fun of other people
Will have their dreams shattered.

I have a dream that people will be selfless
Not selfish.

I have a dream that nobody will scowl or frown
And everyone will have a smile on their face.

I have a dream that our world will be a brighter place
For those who live in it.

I have a dream that the sun will shine
More often.

I have a dream that people will be happy
As they are.

I have a dream that people can have a better life
And nobody starves.

I have a dream that one day these dreams
Will come true.

Samantha Gresty (13)
Walbottle Campus Technology College, Newcastle upon Tyne

I Have A Dream

I have a dream, a dream
Where the grass is green
And the sky is blue
So the clouds are sticky like glue.

I have a dream
Where I'm in the clouds
So high
Even in the never-ending sky.

I have a dream
A dream that I could do whatever I want
Even scream.
There was once a dream
Where I could beam into the night sky
And watch the stars go shooting by.

I have a dream
A dream with cream and cookies
There was a dream
Where I won money at the bookies.

I have a dream that one day
I can drive and be so alive
Then again, I would need to pass my test
So I would have to be the best.

So that's the dream
That I would want to come true
But if not
Then there's always the zoo.

Curtis Hollocks (13)
Walbottle Campus Technology College, Newcastle upon Tyne

I Have A Dream

I have a dream,
But silly it may seem,
My dream is one for peace,
No knife crimes, no guns,
My dream is for happiness,
Life sweet as iced buns.
I never want to see a child cry,
Or hear on the news
Of soldiers that die,
Not hear of kids
Dying at war,
But the sound of our Shearer
Getting us to 6-4.
No killers, no rapists
And no overdosing teens,
No racism and bullying,
You know what I mean.
I want no more fears,
No being scared and no tears.
We should all be the same,
Black or white, young or old,
This is my dream
And I want it to be told.
It's an important dream to me,
I hope that it will come true,
But we'll have to wait and see.
I hope that yours does too!

Stephanie Scott (13)
Walbottle Campus Technology College, Newcastle upon Tyne

120

I Have A Dream

I have a dream that my
Parents were back together
And that I could live with
My mam, dad and brother, so
We could be a happy family again.

I have a dream that I
Could just live in one house
And not going from my mam's
House to my dad's house.

I have a dream that all
Four of us could sit round the
Table again and have a nice
Meal and talk about what
I've done in school today.

I have a dream that we
Could do joyful things
Together again, like going bowling
Or going on a family holiday
To have a good time.

I have a dream that all
That would happen
For even a second
But I know that
Will never be.

Jamie Clayton (12)
Walbottle Campus Technology College, Newcastle upon Tyne

The World Can Change!

I have a dream . . .

People suffering, having bad lives
Nothing else to see but drugs and knives
Racism is the word in a school, in a street
More and more arrests, police on the beat.

Guns and gangs, nothing else to see
We can make a change, just you and me
People grieving and crying every day
Murderers still in public . . . what can I say?

Innocent people getting killed, getting shot
Police cracking the codes, I hope they get the plot
But there is one more problem, one there will always be
Bruises on children from their parents we can see.

My friend's story, one I'll never forget
Every time I hear it, it makes me feel upset . . .

'Me and my dad, the love is gone
All that's left is the fists and rage
My only friend is my covers which I hide under every night.
Stomping upstairs, nothing there but fright
I'd sit there sobbing and hear the shouting
My dad would kill me if he caught me bubbling
I'd then be sleeping all afraid'.

Someone to help him out of that barricade.

Callum Robson (13)
Walbottle Campus Technology College, Newcastle upon Tyne

I Have A Dream

I have a dream
I dream I can be
Anything I want to be

I dream I can fly
With the birds and planes
I dream that I can be
The queen of the sky

I dream I can breathe underwater
To swim with the fish
I dream I can see
The wonders of the Earth and sea

I dream I can be strong
In my heart and soul
I dream I can forgive people
If they do wrong

I dream I can be rich
And able to roll in money
I dream I can be determined
And very hard working

But at this time
I can only dream
And enjoy everything
My life has to bring.

Anna Rogers (13)
Walbottle Campus Technology College, Newcastle upon Tyne

I Have A Dream

He once said, 'I have a dream',
And through the clouds came a sunlight beam.
The crowd parted and there he stood,
Letting them know the things they should.

Passion and freedom
Bellowed out his mouth.
Trying to make his change
To the world right now.

He made them know
We are all the same,
It doesn't matter about our race.

We may sound different,
Our looks may change,
We could even believe in different things.

But his message states loud and clear,
For everyone to achieve and hear.

You might still hear it ringing round,
All races, all colours know it somehow.
From the highest mountain
To the lowest valley,
I have a dream you will hear someday.

Jamie Dobson (13)
Walbottle Campus Technology College, Newcastle upon Tyne

The Soldier

Sitting in the scalding heat with nothing to eat,
Don't like the chief, who says we need a new fleet,
I can't wait to get home, so I can organise a trip to Rome
I hate my job, it's always sad, I need to leave or I will bleed,
Sitting alone with no way home, all I have is a short poem.

Philip Stevenson (13)
Walbottle Campus Technology College, Newcastle upon Tyne

The Dream Poem

I had a dream,
A dream that I had,
About a man dreaming,
Dreaming a better dream,
Dreaming of a better tomorrow.

Tomorrow he dreamed,
The better dream he dreamed about,
The dream he had dreamed,
Was nothing like this other dream,
Because this was now better
Than yesterday's dream.

But Monday's dream
Was better than Thursday's dream,
Even though it was now
Better than Friday's dream.
Which got him thinking
Of the dreams he had
On Tuesday, Wednesday and Saturday.

So on Sunday
He got dreaming
And that dream was about . . .

Jonathan Tindall (13)
Walbottle Campus Technology College, Newcastle upon Tyne

I Have A Dream

I wish for world peace.
I wish black and white people could get along.
I wish everything was clean.
I had a dream that I wish could come true.

Stacey Calvert (12)
Walbottle Campus Technology College, Newcastle upon Tyne

I Have A Dream

I wish no smoking,
I wish no more drugs because
It is so silly.

1, 2, 3, 4, 5,
With the drugs you're not alive,
6, 7, 8, 9, 10,
Do not take them again and again.
Off to the hospital you go,
Learning what not to do,
So don't take them, right?
Then everything will be alright.

A knife, a knife,
It could mess up your life.
A dagger, a dagger,
It'll kill you, no matter.
A gun, a gun,
You can't run.
A sniper, a sniper,
It'll make you hyper.

No knives, no drugs, no wars, no guns,
This is my dream.

Robert Lowes (12)
Walbottle Campus Technology College, Newcastle upon Tyne

I Have A Dream

I have a dream to see no more
The animal cruelty within,
To stop the suffering and starvation
And violent attacks and abandonment.

I have a dream that every animal
Will have a happy place
To run and jump and bark and play,
To have a good life forever.

To see the things that I've seen
Is more than a frightening shock,
To see the things that I've seen
Will make your body rock with terror.

From young to old,
From healthy to ill,
From life to death,
From home to streets,

If we try and help them in every way,
There will surely be a chance.

Yes, that's my dream!

Laura Watts (12)
Walbottle Campus Technology College, Newcastle upon Tyne

I Have A Dream

I have a dream
There will be a world
In peace and without war
And no pollution from a car.

I have a dream
Children will live in happiness
And no one will be racist.

I have a dream
Everyone will live in harmony
And not poverty.

I have a dream
Where no one is rich
And no one poor
So everyone can live
With a front door.

I have a dream
No one will become ill
And if you do
There will be a cure in a pill.

Beth Knox (13)
Walbottle Campus Technology College, Newcastle upon Tyne

I Have A Dream

I have a dream where no violence is allowed
And everyone will stand proud,
I have a dream where racism will stop,
And everyone will stand on top,
I have a dream where religions don't fight,
Where it doesn't matter if you're black or white,
I have a dream of no crime,
Where criminals will vanish in time.
I have a dream where life will be fine.

Rebecca Tearney (12)
Walbottle Campus Technology College, Newcastle upon Tyne

I Have A Dream

I have a dream to buy a horse
And jump him in a jumping course.
I have a dream to do well,
To canter away on the bell.

I have a dream to gallop,
To gallop along the seaside edge.
I have a dream the sea will cover,
Cover up my horse's tracks.

I have a dream to buy a horse
And jump him in a jumping course.
I have a dream to do well,
To canter away on the bell.

I have a dream,
To groom and clean.

I have a dream,
We'll be the perfect team.

But most importantly, I have a dream,
That this dream will come true!

Jessica Mae Ridley (12)
Walbottle Campus Technology College, Newcastle upon Tyne

I Have A Dream

I have a dream to drive a racing car
And drive it really fast.
I have a dream to be a Formula 1 driver.
I have a dream to travel the world
And to see everything there is to see.
I have a dream to have a successful job
And to have a big house and to be rich.
I have a dream.

Scott Robinson (12)
Walbottle Campus Technology College, Newcastle upon Tyne

129

I Have A Dream

I have a dream that we can all be friends, be friends, be friends,
Be friends to the end and may it mend each other's hearts
So we can be all together as one.
No one will fight and kill, I for one will stand up and stand still.
I stand still in this war, seeing the death of one in front of my eyes
And another will soon cease to be.
I for one still have a dream.
I have a dream that this will stop,
I have a dream that we will help,
I have a dream that this war will end
And that there will be no more death.
So help the poor and give them food,
Help them now and then we can go on,
Go on, go on, to give them food.
Give them food and drink and with those who cease to be,
Let them rest in peace.
I have a dream that we can do it.
I have a dream that we will stop and bring peace to the world.
So let's hold hands and give our love,
Because I have a dream that we can give our love to the world.

Kathryn Needham (12)
Walbottle Campus Technology College, Newcastle upon Tyne

I Have A Dream

I have a dream that the world
Will become a better place.

I have a dream that there will be
A cure for cancer.

I have a dream that people should
Get a second chance at life.

I have a dream that we could live forever
And never get old.

I have a dream there would be
No such thing as crime.

I have a dream that everyone
Saw beyond skin colour.

I have a dream that I could visit
The people in Heaven.

I have a dream that all these dreams
Will come true.

Rebecca Lackenby (12)
Walbottle Campus Technology College, Newcastle upon Tyne

I Have A Dream

I have a dream
That I can jump so high,
So high I can touch the sky,
Where birds fly by.

I have a dream
That I can drive a car,
Drive it very far.

I have a dream
That I could fly,
Fly higher than the light blue sky.

Shaan Sadiq (12)
Walbottle Campus Technology College, Newcastle upon Tyne

I Have A Dream, A Big One!

Someone is courageous,
Walking on the streets,
At precisely 9 o'clock,
When all the under society are out and about,
There by the corner shop,
Jumping in and out,
Making the automatics go crazy in the head,
They're eyeing up the booze, looking behind the counter,
Here he comes, let's get him,
The thoughts that come to their mind,
Let's rob his pension pocket,
Just like we did last week, week, week.

But I, yes I, have a dream to stop all this,
Like making the neighbourhood safer
And let everyone be safe,
With no muggings or attacks
And no abuse or violence.

I have a dream, a big one!

Daniel Percy (12)
Walbottle Campus Technology College, Newcastle upon Tyne

Bullies Are Mean!

I have a dream that there would be no more bullies
And everyone is nice to each other.
No more bullying would be better for everyone.
Victims who get bullied feel very upset
And that happened to someone I met.
Just be nice with some sugar and spice.
Bullies are mean, so don't be mean,
Because you would be a nasty thing.

It doesn't matter about your height,
Or if you're right.

Megan Satterthwaite (12)
Walbottle Campus Technology College, Newcastle upon Tyne

I Have A Dream

I have a dream to be free,
To live a life that I can see,
I have a dream to live a life
Without a gun or knife in sight,
I have a dream of worldwide peace,
To have a nephew and a niece
Who see my dream and help to make it real.

I have a dream to live my dream
And travel around the world,
I have a dream to be a worldwide sensation,
A writer, an artist, a poet,
I have a dream of a world without war,
To have a world where no one saw
The pain and punishment of bullying and crime.

I have a dream
That the world will one day make peace.

I have a dream!

Toni Lockey (11)
Walbottle Campus Technology College, Newcastle upon Tyne

He Had A Dream

He had a dream and it came true,
But for his family the pain just grew,
For on the 4th of April 1968,
Martin Luther King died
And his wife and kids sat down and cried.
But they know he didn't die in vain,
For his dream came true and took away the pain.
41 years and his dream still stays
And people have forgotten the cruel days.
He's probably in Heaven watching over us
And making sure no one has to sit at the front of the bus!

Calvin Fletcher (13)
Walbottle Campus Technology College, Newcastle upon Tyne

I Have A Dream

I have a dream that one day the tears will dry up
And the fighting will fade.
No more bruises, just a tan on a sunny day.
You look around and all you will see is people smiling happily,
With rings of laughter instead of moans and sighs.
No more badness, that has all died and gone.
Until the winter returns it will come back.
The sun will shine, the grass will grow,
That's all you need on a summer's day, that and fun!

Winter days are the worst,
The tears all flood back, the smiles drop into frowns
And moans and sighs return.
Everyone gets aggressive, like dogs
They need to get put on leads.
The suntan fades and is replaced with black and blue marks.
By then you know the bullies have returned to hurt you, but worse.

What do you prefer?

Melissa Eggleton (13)
Walbottle Campus Technology College, Newcastle upon Tyne

I Have A Dream

I wish no more war,
Shooting, killing, wailing gun shells
Hitting the ground like ringing bells.
Destroying the sky with their evil weapons
Falling one by one, will it ever stop?
Killing the sea with turrets of death
Sinking to the fishes' bed.
No war! No war!
Peace is the way.
That is the greatest dream.

Adam Bolton (12)
Walbottle Campus Technology College, Newcastle upon Tyne

Life, Love And Peace

I have a dream that one day there will be no war
And that everyone will be equal.
Fat or thin, black or white, straight or gay
And that I can walk down the street
And not be followed or chased.
I dream of my future, will I have a good future?
Not of drugs and alcohol.
That there will be no lies and that when you see someone
You won't get out a knife,
You'll stop and say hello.

I have a dream for peace
That instead of people making bombs and weapons
They will make the tables and chairs that we sit on
To negotiate, discuss and forgive.
I dream of illness,
Will I get ill or die at a young age?

I dream of life.

Alex Greenup (13)
Walbottle Campus Technology College, Newcastle upon Tyne

I Have A Dream

I have a dream that there are no more lies,
About the little children who give their cries.
Every day they get abused
And at school they just get used.
They get treated like nobody cares,
When they get home, they're thrown down the stairs.
They clamber to bed full of pain and sorrow
And dream about a life with a better tomorrow.
Help these children who give their cries,
Stop them living a life of lies.

Amy Hedley (13)
Walbottle Campus Technology College, Newcastle upon Tyne

I Have A Dream

I have a dream
That there are no things bad such as abuse.
I have a dream
Where everyone has money that we wouldn't lose.
I have a dream
Where smoking is banned for life.
I have a dream where no one lies.

I have a dream
Where the sky is always blue.
I have a dream where there are no drugs for you
Or anyone there!
Because it isn't fair on the people
Who are trying to live, love life.
I have a dream that people won't judge you
For what you look like.
I have a dream,
I have lots of dreams.

Hannah May (11)
Walbottle Campus Technology College, Newcastle upon Tyne

I Have A Dream

I have a dream

H ope will come
A nd peace will stay
V iolence is over
E nvironment is better

A nimals won't be extinct

D reams will come true
R oads will be opened
E nergy is saved
A nd we have a better life
M aybe it will come true.

Savannah Hogarth (11)
Walbottle Campus Technology College, Newcastle upon Tyne

Dreamy!

I have a dream that . . .
I could fly . . . fly far away
Build my own house
And live there every day!

I have a dream that I
Saw a shooting star
Made my wish
Which was granted from afar.

I had a dream
That I had wings
To fly above
And look down on everything.

I had a dream that my wishes
Came true
Until then
I'll keep them in my view.

Amy Fay (12)
Walbottle Campus Technology College, Newcastle upon Tyne

I Have A Dream

I have a dream,
That there's no school,
Now that would be cool.
I have a dream,
That there will be no violence,
Just peace and silence.

I have a dream,
That I can fly,
Through the clouds in the sky.
I have a dream,
I don't have to get out of bed,
With my pillow touching my head.

Matthew Bould (13)
Walbottle Campus Technology College, Newcastle upon Tyne

End Cruelty To Animals

Not treated right
Left in an alley
This one was called Sally
Big and strong
But treated wrong
Left in the cold
With no one to hold

But then came help
In the most unlikely place
They took her in
And gave her space

Sally is now living happily
With her new family

You can help other animals
Just by at least giving 50p
To the RSPCA.

Kieron Smith Fairley (13)
Walbottle Campus Technology College, Newcastle upon Tyne

I Have A Dream . . .

I have a dream to be a multi millionaire
I want to give money to charity
I want to settle war
I want to do more.

I want to give money to families in need
I want to visit Africa
I want to give money and help slaves be freed.

I want to put effort into stopping poverty
I want to help the government battle the recession.

After I have done this I won't have millions
But I will still feel like a multi millionaire.

Ryan Anderson (12)
Walbottle Campus Technology College, Newcastle upon Tyne

Jack's War!

Lying on the beach in Iraq,
Ten troops remaining, one called Jack.
'Fire at will!' the sergeant says,
Londoner Jack says, 'Oh my days!'

Bang! Bang! Bang! Jack's pulling the trigger,
Killing more people than Jack the Ripper.
Backwards and forwards the bullets come,
Britain's army nearly all gone.

I have a dream this war will stop,
It's like a routine aim, lock and shot,
One man down, the next one dead,
Iraqi bullet straight through Jack's head.

Blood is trickling down the beach,
Everybody looks and they're lost for speech.
All the wars are dead and gone,
No more bullets, no more bombs!

Liam Burns (13)
Walbottle Campus Technology College, Newcastle upon Tyne

I Have A Dream

I have a dream that the world is fair
And everyone is equal,
Hopefully, this poem won't need a sequel.

No more poverty, murders or abuse,
No more killers should ever be let loose.

Drugs, knives and guns will all fade away
And nobody will ever have a bad day.

I had a dream that everybody said *stop*,
To all the killers, abusers and all the racists
And the world was a better place
And everyone was happy all of the time.

Dan Harrison (12)
Walbottle Campus Technology College, Newcastle upon Tyne

139

I Have A Dream

I have a dream
That the grass will be green
The sky won't be grey
And everyone will get along
One day.

I have a dream
Black will be white
Like yin and yang
And everyone will be alright.

Like a fish to water
A bird to the sky
I wish I could fly away
Just for the day.

Away from racism
Away from spite
Is there anywhere I can spend the night?

Corey Watson (13)
Walbottle Campus Technology College, Newcastle upon Tyne

I Have A Dream

I   have a dream

H ave a dream for no trouble
A   dream for no pollution
V iolence is not the answer
E verybody is at peace.

A   wonderful world, no more

D angerous actions
R acism is no more
E verybody gets along
A nd no more wars
M y world would be perfect.

Nicole Coulthard (12)
Walbottle Campus Technology College, Newcastle upon Tyne

I Have A Dream

I have a dream
That all waters are blue
And all people have faith.

I have a dream
That violence and racism
Never existed.

I have a dream
That people act maturely
And do not terrorise our planet
That bombs were never thought of
And people have a guilty conscience
About what they are going to do.

I have a dream
That all smidges
And smudges and bangs and bombs
Are just left out of life completely.

Caitlyn Howitt (12)
Walbottle Campus Technology College, Newcastle upon Tyne

I Have A Dream

I have a dream that

H urt is no more and
A nger is not a feeling
V iolence is gone and
E very man and woman are equal

A nd all the wars are over

D reams take over nightmares
R acism is over and
E very religion is the same
A nd guns are no more because
M y dream is a peaceful dream.

Adam Hoole (12)
Walbottle Campus Technology College, Newcastle upon Tyne

I Have A Dream

I have a dream
Standing on the stage
Singing songs
At a young age!

I have a dream
Shooting a ball
Into the air
And into the goal!

I have a dream
Where the world is peaceful
All are having fun
Where the world is beautiful.

I have a dream
That the violence had walked away
Seeing sense
And wasn't here to stay!

Laura Glenwright (11)
Walbottle Campus Technology College, Newcastle upon Tyne

I Have A Dream

I have a dream of

H elping the poor
A nd stopping gun crime
V iolence stopped and being
E nvironmentally healthy

A nd in my world I

D ream that
R acism stops
E veryone healthy and
A ll people wealthy
M y world would be perfect.

Jason Miller (11)
Walbottle Campus Technology College, Newcastle upon Tyne

I Have A Dream

I have a dream that everyone
Will be treated the same,
No matter if you're black or white
Or the sound of your name.

I think that even if
You're young or old,
Your important opinion
Should always be told.

It doesn't matter where you come from
Or where you are now,
You should always be respected
Someway and somehow.

And no one can tell you
What you should do,
You should always be yourself
And remember that too.

Hope Armstrong (12)
Walbottle Campus Technology College, Newcastle upon Tyne

I Have A Dream

I have a dream to see shooting stars
And have a relative that drives racing cars.

I have a dream to play in a band
And get loud applause from my fans.

I have a dream that I'm invisible
And have loads of confidence to speak out loud.

I have a dream that there are no regrets
And nothing to get off your chest.

I have a dream that the world is all well . . .

I have a dream!

Aimee Shorter (12)
Walbottle Campus Technology College, Newcastle upon Tyne

143

I Have A Dream

I have a dream . . .

I have a dream that one day I will travel the world,
To go and see all the boys and girls
Who are too dehydrated to survive,
And those who are lucky to still be alive

I have a hope . . .

I have a hope that one day I will help these children,
Who are in need of food and water,
To build a shelter and give them warmth,
So they don't suffer from the cold.

Imagine . . .

Imagine if I helped the children to live a happy life,
To show them what it's like
To be loved and cared for,
And make them safe, the poor little mites.

Jennifer Massey (13)
Walbottle Campus Technology College, Newcastle upon Tyne

I Have A Dream

I have a dream that guns will be no more,
That climate change will just blow away
And no trace will be left.
I have a dream that hatred and violence
Will not be an option,
That the world will know
What to do in desperate needs.
I have a dream that black and white
Will always stay positive to one another,
Even though they are not the same,
Like the Earth and wind.
My dream is for a better world in peace.

Jordan Collins (12)
Walbottle Campus Technology College, Newcastle upon Tyne

144

I Have A Dream

I have a dream
A dream that I can be anything I want to be.

A dream that I will never stop
I can do anything if I put my mind to it
I will reach the top.

I won't just sit around
I will do everything I can
To be where I want to be.

I dream I will be happy whatever I do
And I will live my life exactly how I want to.

Because I am free
To be me.

I believe in myself
And no one else
I can be whoever I want to be.

Sarah Docherty (13)
Walbottle Campus Technology College, Newcastle upon Tyne

Say No To War

Say no to war
It's not good
Why do we fight?
No need at all
Stop the war
I have a dream
That the world will live in peace
I have a dream
That children and their families won't suffer any more
I have a dream.

Laura-Beth Ridley (13)
Walbottle Campus Technology College, Newcastle upon Tyne

Untitled

I had the greatest dream
It could make people scream

No more black and no more white
Let that be clear day and night

No more bullies, no more threats
No more bankrupt, no more debt.

More sports and more sports games
No more poor and no more fame.

No more ugly and no more pretty
No more selfish and no more witty.

No more hatred, no more illness
No more suffering, more forgiveness.

Let us have a lot more love,
Let's stay peaceful like a dove.

Daniel Sopp (13)
Walbottle Campus Technology College, Newcastle upon Tyne

I Have A Dream

This is a poem for children
Whose parents have gone their separate ways,
Wishing that their dad would just stay.
Sobbing their heart out
Wishing it's not true,
Just hope that their parents know
That it involves them too.
They think to themselves
That it is all their fault,
They can't go downstairs,
Who is at fault?
They just want to be happily every after,
But why should it not be all smiles and laughter?

Kate Swarbrick (13)
Walbottle Campus Technology College, Newcastle upon Tyne

I Have A Dream

I have a dream . . .
I have a dream that poverty will stop
I have a dream that whales aren't thrown in a pot
I have a dream that war will stop
I have a dream that the poor could grow crops
I have a dream that racists should be shot
I have a dream . . .

I have a dream . . .
I have a dream that white and black can sit in the same room
I have a dream that they will think in the same tune
I have a dream that animals aren't chained up
I have a dream that countries won't erupt
I have a dream that disease is cured with ease
I have a dream that animals aren't killed
I have a dream that these aren't used for our bellies to be filled
I have a dream . . .

Alex Black (12)
Walbottle Campus Technology College, Newcastle upon Tyne

I Have A Dream

I have a dream . . .
I want things to change
So the world is fair
I want all the negative things
To just disappear.
I want the world to be amazing.

I have a dream . . .
I have a wish
For there to be no war
So we live in peace
For the rest of our lives.

I have a wish . . .

Sarah Wightman (12)
Walbottle Campus Technology College, Newcastle upon Tyne

147

I Have A Dream

I have a dream
Abuse is no more,
Because their nightmare waits behind the door.
Give them a life, a chance, some hope,
For all they do is sit and mope.
They curl up in the dirt,
All battered and hurt.
They feel unwanted, unloved, ashamed,
Anything that happens, they get blamed.
Their parents sit all comfy and warm,
They sit in the cold, their clothes all torn.
I have a dream that this has all ended,
There's no more abuse, lives are mended.
I have a dream, please hear me out,
I don't want to hear another scream or shout.
I have a dream, so let's make this happen!

Sophie Moran-Wrightson (12)
Walbottle Campus Technology College, Newcastle upon Tyne

Peace

I have a dream,
That all will be well,
Countries will stop fighting
And we will bring peace to God's creation.

We don't deserve to be punished
For racism and crime,
Immigration will not be a problem,
As we stand up for what we believe in.

We will unite as one,
As our people smile and cheer,
We say a job well done,
I have a dream!

Nicole Sams (13)
Walbottle Campus Technology College, Newcastle upon Tyne

148

I Have A Dream

There I lay in a ditch so dim
Cold and hungry yet so thin
Scrounging for money night and day
Hoping for someone to carry me away.

For once right now, I have a dream
Just for one day to be so clean
As now I am filled with grazes and cuts
Mainly on the bottom of my size 5 feet.

I have no socks, yet no shoes
Many people relate me as Zulus
I have no hopes and yet no dreams
I don't exist as that would seem.

But now I am 20 and still no home
Maybe it's time for me to go.

Christopher Porrett (13)
Walbottle Campus Technology College, Newcastle upon Tyne

I Have A Dream

I have a dream,
I dream to make the world around us a better place,
To have no racism or wars,
To let all the light shine on us and make us all equal,
Some day there will be no more poverty
And make all our lives happier a little bit more.

I have a dream,
To make sure that everyone gets a good education,
That everyone smiles at least three times a day,
Doesn't everyone deserve a chance in this world?
Everyone gives something to help others,
To make other people's dreams come true,
Do you have a dream?
I have a dream.

Amy Roberts (13)
Walbottle Campus Technology College, Newcastle upon Tyne

149

The Simple Dream

Sitting, sobbing, afraid,
Cold, lonely it waits.
Love, the only thing left,
It reaches TV.
The bubbling rage,
Shout, find,
Little dog waits.
Found! Causing a big debate!
Hunted down, caught,
The courtroom decide their fate.
Unfair judgement I honestly think,
It happens again before I blink!
I have a dream, a simple one,
I hate animal cruelty,
It should be gone!

Jonn Gallon (13)
Walbottle Campus Technology College, Newcastle upon Tyne

I Have A Dream

I have a dream
That there will be no wrong in the world,
A world where there is no murder, crime or war,
A world where everyone is equal,
Black or white, fat or thin, gay or straight,
A world where no one is judged by appearance
Or personality.
I have a dream for a peaceful world
With no violence,
No need for police or ambulances,
A dream where you can walk down the street
Without being shouted at because of your religion,
A world where there are no bombs or weapons.

I have a dream.

Ben Ramshaw (12)
Walbottle Campus Technology College, Newcastle upon Tyne

Orphan

I have a dream
A dream to be loved
I'm just a small child
Left free to run wild
My mother doesn't want me
My father doesn't care
Both of them pretend like I'm not even there
I sleep on the floor
Cold, next to the door
The school kids tease
So help me please
I'm hungry, not fed
My parents wish I was dead
I'm always alone
Please find me a home.

Katie Sibbald (13)
Walbottle Campus Technology College, Newcastle upon Tyne

I Have A Dream

I have a dream that the human race
Is living in a better place.

In the world everyone cares
And everyone has equal shares.

Poverty will be no more,
It would disappear and so would war.

Nobody is judged by how they look,
Not like the cover of a book.

With no more guns and no more knives,
Everyone would lead safer lives.

What a good world it would be for me and you,
If only this world was really true.

Rachael Bolton (13)
Walbottle Campus Technology College, Newcastle upon Tyne

I Have A Dream

I have a dream of no violence,
I have a dream of world peace,
I have a dream of no crimes
And life would be a bliss.

I have a dream of no racism,
I have a dream of happiness,
I have a dream of no lies
And everyone opens their eyes,
To see the world needs to change
Now or never,
Today, not tomorrow.

I have a dream of life in the future
And when we make this change,
These are my dreams, I hope they come true.

Abbie Telford (12)
Walbottle Campus Technology College, Newcastle upon Tyne

I Have A Dream

I have a dream
All wars will end
All racism will end
All fat people will not be judged
All thin people will not be judged
All gay people will not be judged
What people wear will be unimportant
Everybody will be respected
Everybody is paid enough to live
Everybody has enough food to live
Everybody lives in a safe environment
Every animal has respect and care
I have a dream that many people ignore
I have a dream, but it's a dream and not real life.

Gary Philipson (13)
Walbottle Campus Technology College, Newcastle upon Tyne

I Have A Dream

I have a dream to end the wars
I hate them, they involve blood and gore.
End racism,
End bullying,
End them,
I hate them.
Blood and gore lead to death, hatred,
Betrayal,
Friends are lying,
People dying,
Everyone crying,
Stop!
I have a dream,
I hope it comes true.

Daniel Laws (12)
Walbottle Campus Technology College, Newcastle upon Tyne

I Have A Dream

I have a dream
To be a jet fighter pilot
I'd like to fly in the air a lot
Equal rights for black and white
If you smoke your chest goes tight.

End the war
Help the poor
Get rid of drugs
You stupid mugs.

Stop the violence
Let's pick violets
End it now
I'll take you down.

Adam Anderson-Brown (11)
Walbottle Campus Technology College, Newcastle upon Tyne

153

I Have A Dream

I have a dream to be free as a bird,
Apparently they're free, that's what I've heard.
I am happy when I am free,
Being free pleases me.

I want to travel the world and see the sights,
I want to go caving and climb the heights.
I want to go my own way and have some fun,
I want to do work in the boiling sun.

I have a dream to be free,
Some day it will happen to me.
My dream is unfolding and that's just fine,
I hope I can fulfil this dream of mine.

Kate Miller (12)
Walbottle Campus Technology College, Newcastle upon Tyne

Running Free

In my dream the world will be
Wild with horses running free,
Hooves that thunder across the ground,
Among the men they can be found.

In my dream this world we'll share,
The green, green grass and the summer air.
Free together, roaming free,
This is where I want to be.

In my dream they won't be ridden,
They never have to stay forbidden.
Horse and man will share this land,
Stand together hoof and hand.

Lucy Gales (12)
Walbottle Campus Technology College, Newcastle upon Tyne

I Have A Dream

A dream that drugs do not exist
It's already happened in Ireland, why not here as well?
I hope they are banned, yes I do insist,
That is my dream.

You take them once and you are addicted,
Take them twice and you are dead.
If you do not die, you will go off your head,
If you are not off your head, you will be dead.

I hope my dream comes true.

Ben Crawford (11)
Walbottle Campus Technology College, Newcastle upon Tyne

My Dream

I train at gymnastics five times a week
I try to come first in competitions where I compete
But no matter how hard I try
I think of my dreams and how much more I can fly.

I dream all night, I dream all day
I think of what the judges would say
When I step up onto the floor
Hopefully they will want to see more.

They let me go on to join the champions.

I face the judges once again
They've all been champions in their days
But now it's my turn to show my stuff
It goes so quickly, like a puff.

They give me first, I'm amazed
That's what I dream, that's what I gaze
That's what I want to do in future days
To be champion of champions.
    That's *my dream!*

Emily Parker (12)
Whitburn CE School, Sunderland

The Universe And The Cosmos

The cosmos, the universe and the wonders I see,
This is what inspires me.
From the deep black holes to the core of the sun,
It was a tiny place from where this had begun.

From the smallest of seeds,
Grows the largest of trees.

Through history people have pondered how the universe got here,
Some ideas are good, some plain weird.
Though all these ideas have gone through,
Some of them could still be true.

According to the Bible, God created the world in six days,
But there are a variety of other ways.
Greeks believe the world was created by many gods
of which chaos was the dad,
That is thought to be slightly mad.
But the Egyptians believed that life was spoken by a god called Ra -
That is pushing it a bit too far.

From the smallest of seeds,
Grows the largest of trees.

But science has spoken and it has said
That the universe began from an area the size of a pinhead
And over millions of years the galaxies came,
Since then the world was never the same.

From the smallest of seeds,
Grows the largest of trees.

Nebula, galaxies, planets and deep space,
The universe is an amazing place,
A place full of wonders, a complex design
And there is a lot to find.

From the smallest of seeds,
Grows the largest of trees.

The size of the universe is truly amazing,
It is very inspiring.
Our planet Earth, including all of us,
In the universe is a speck of dust.

From the smallest of seeds,
Grows the largest of trees.

The universe, with all of its wonders to see,
This is what inspires me.
With its complexity,
For all life to see.

There have been some questions, it's been said,
From which some great answers have been read.
There is one question never to be forgot,
Are we alone in the universe or not?

Jacob Baxter (12)
Whitburn CE School, Sunderland

Golden Footprints

Footprints padding along the shore,
The waves crashing for evermore,
The clouds are gathering,
The night draws in; darkness all around,
People are whispering; an echoing sound,
The sun begins to set and sparks the sky alight,
The fiery colours burning all through the night,
Like a thousand dreams aflame . . .

Whose voices are they that whisper on icy shores?
Whose dreams are set on fire?
The seagulls cry from high above,
The footprints lead on across the sands
To some foreign, unknown land.

Do they find their destiny?
Do they reach their goals?
Who knows?
All there's left is to wonder,
And walk the sands of gold,
The dreams and memories left untold
Are marked by a golden footprint.

Sophie Brownson (14)
Whitburn CE School, Sunderland

I Have A Dream Poem

I have a dream,
We can live throughout all,
So that no man or woman is mean,
So we can go into a hall
Where there are no arguments,
And all have peace,
So we can give it up for Lent
And live in a society like the French town, Nice.

I go to a school,
Where all is fair,
So there are no fools
And there are no liars,
Only people who believe,
So they can go and see
And forget and leave,
Those who don't believe they can go leave me.

I live in a society
That can be whole
And live with variety,
Rather than be a small mole.
We can look at the past,
And think fast and good,
We all know it's been a blast,
We will think on our past which has been bloody.

I will leave the world on a note,
This will prove our life,
This will reflect on hope,
Where there were no knives,
Where I realise my dream
Came true,
Not to be mean,
But as it was all true,
It was a fantastic ride,
Where all was right and no wrong,
But we don't hide,
It ended with a big bang!

Alistair Parry (12)
Whitburn CE School, Sunderland

The Changing Faces Of The Sea

I look down at the sea below,
I am an old nautical lover,
I look down at the sea below,
What secrets can I discover?

The blistering sun glistening on the still, turquoise sea,
Whilst jellyfish and stingrays gracefully glide around me,
The multicoloured tropical fish dart erratically in flight,
Friendly, leaping dolphins are such a beautiful sight.

I look down at the sea below,
I am an old nautical lover,
I look down at the sea below,
What secrets can I discover?

Black clouds begin to cover the sun and are ready to start sobbing,
White horses rise from the deep blue sea and their heads are bobbing,
Lobsters and crabs scurry for safety under rocks and sand,
Wise, old sea lions beckon their young to safe land.

I look down at the sea below,
I am an old nautical lover,
I look down at the sea below,
What secrets can I discover?

Thunderous, black skies and flashes of violent, streak lightning,
A cold, cruel, dark sea and crashing tidal waves are frightening!
In the turmoil, killer sharks hunt madly for their prey,
Unfortunate sailors find Davy Jones' locker and forever stay.

I look down at the sea below,
I am an old nautical lover,
I look down at the sea below,
Where there are many secrets to discover!

Christopher Nixon (11)
Whitburn CE School, Sunderland

159

I Have A Dream

I have a dream, a long-lasting, amazing and exciting dream.
We live in a beautiful world of comfort and love,
Everyone is kind and caring, happy and sharing.
People are treated equally and fairly,
At last the world not so scary.
Whatever colour or creed, disability or need,
A life of joy for every girl and boy.
Life is created to enjoy;
Peace and harmony among us all,
Sister and brother, father and mother,
We all love one another.
No stealing or sadness,
No murder or madness.
People are fascinated by school,
By learning and education,
It inspires the nation.
People care for one another,
Like a sister and a brother.
This dream is just perfect,
No need to be checked,
All wrongs in life are put right,
All opportunities looking bright.
I didn't want it to end,
There was nothing to amend.
A perfect world,
Life beginning to be unfurled.
Why can't the world be like my dream?
I really, really could scream!
My other dream, is that this dream,
One day will not just only be a dream!

Lauren McNally (11)
Whitburn CE School, Sunderland

Moving On

The ocean blue looks up at you
And then you think of things that are new
And wonder where time has gone.

As time flew by
Like a bird in the sky
The damp, dark, winter days die
And summer soon approaches.

The lazy days filled with sun
All day long it's fun, fun, fun
But time soon catches up again
And then it goes back to where it began.

New people, new faces, new chances to be had
But when it's all over, I will soon be glad
You see this life is too hectic for me
All I want is to let it be.

Maybe one day I will be great
Maybe one day I will change the world
But at the moment
I am content.

I live in a world where I could do anything
Yet some choose to do nothing
I will try to make this world better
And I will try to leave my mark
I will try to be good
And I will try to be smart.

Zach Casey (15)
Whitburn CE School, Sunderland

What Can You See?

Seas, what can you see?
The race of men to and fro,
The gents of women moving slow,
Playful children sailing away,
Playful toddlers enjoying day.

Man, what can you see?
The tidal ebb and tidal flow,
The marine life gently go
About their business, night and day,
Wasting the universe of time away.

World, what can you see?
The human race wasting away,
With global warming topic of the day,
Traffic, traffic all the way,
Stretching as far as San Francisco Bay.

Universe, what can you see?
Planet Earth turning red,
Planet Earth lying near dead,
Planet Earth's turn to decay,
Planet Earth's time fading away.

Me, what can I see?
I can see the human race
Falling, falling out of place,
Carbon dioxide fills the air,
While only some seem to care.

Robert Staincliffe (15)
Whitburn CE School, Sunderland

Star Child

If a child is born to darkness, then only shadows they would know,
The dreary, sullen obscurity of society and so,
When the radiance of a star glows a little bright,
The realisation comes that existence can be bright.

Stars are made from dead rocks, though there's nothing more alive,
Than the fiery fusion explosions; desire and strong mind.
First the tiny pieces must collect and then ignite,
So in some towns of darkness there shines the brightest light.

I've seen these kind of people littered in my sky,
Sometimes a spectacular comet will just go shooting by.
But when I'm in the city, the irony is this,
More people; more opportunity yet more stars are amiss.

Perhaps it's because they're hiding or maybe just can't glow through
The dimness of the city life, so they wait before they can prove
How they can change a world for good, maybe yours or mine,
To give us a chance to be the moon reflecting gold sunshine.

Rocks are only seen on Earth if they are surrounded by golden rays
Yet if you're stumbling around in darkness, there must be another way,
For every rock holds potential to illuminate right,
Nothing in existence was born wrong, the proof you'll see at night.

Hush as babies sleeping; sigh as the sun makes dawn
I still can feel my stars are watching, to help me when forlorn.
They each give me guidance and help me with my life,
They stick around to comfort me when immense threat is rife.

Emma Rees (14)
Whitburn CE School, Sunderland

Imagine

Imagine all the people
Living all their dreams,
Imagine all the people
Making them reality.

I have a dream of all dreams
That peace is a reality,
And that people live
In prosperous harmony.

People have genuine inspiration
That is what Martin Luther King said.
'I have a dream', with this he inspired generations,
With great people at its head.

Imagine there is no Heaven,
Even if you don't try.
Dreams make the world
Just drift on by.

People call me a dreamer,
But when they join us too,
Then the world will be one,
Just like me and you.

People are not people without their dreams,
Dreams make the reality
And in the heart of this wonderful dream,
There is a dazed dreamer, just like me!

Liam Mattimore (12)
Whitburn CE School, Sunderland

I Have A Dream

I have a dream,
To be a gymnast that is outstanding,
We do floor, vault, bars and beam,
Although the sport is very demanding.

Vault is all about power,
Strength and focus too,
You have to be balanced as a tower,
Or marks are taken off you.

Beam is all about balance,
You have a mount,
Difficult moves and dance
And to round off the routine, dismount.

Floor is all about showing off the tumbles,
But the dance is important as well,
Judges not impressed with stumbles,
You really have to excel.

Bars is all about concentration and strength,
You have the momentum on your side,
Doing the giants to full length,
But sometimes you can slip and slide.

I have a dream,
To be a gymnast that is outstanding,
We do floor, vault, bars and beam,
Although the sport is very demanding.

Amy Whitehead (11)
Whitburn CE School, Sunderland

My Life And Dreams

I believe dreams can come true,
I believe I can turn the sky crystal blue.

My miracles lead to peace,
My freedom will never cease.

School is my inspiration,
My happiness, love and joy,
My life used to be isolation,
Our new school is not a toy.

Fortune is fortune,
That will never change,
I will be a Year 8 soon,
My life will never rearrange.

I don't know what I want to be,
A Hollywood star?
A dancer maybe?
Whatever I do I want to go far.

My ambition is to get a degree,
For everyone to take credit from me.

I have a dream, one day some of it will come true,
A passion, ambition, fortune, inspiration, dream,
One day it may be you.
I want to be part of the scheme.

Rachel Moody (11)
Whitburn CE School, Sunderland

I Have A Dream

To see the world from a human eye
To see the world from the eye of a fly
It doesn't matter who it is
It's important all the same
The problem is, do we want to see it?

Emily Henderson (13)
Whitburn CE School, Sunderland

166

Inspiration?

What makes us happy, willing and glad?
What puts persistency into precise?
What keeps us going when we are sad?
Which secretly gives us advice
Without the thought of a price?

What comes and goes in a flash?
What takes our life and makes a bend?
What ups the money and the cash?
What stays with us until our end
And after we do ascend?

Not by money or material things
But by the people who do good deeds,
We may worship them like kings
But we too have human needs,
Which drives us onwards,
They are our guiding leads
So that we can also plant this seed.

I'm talking, of course, about something we all feel,
Whether we are actors or shop assistants
That both do different things,
We cannot see it, but it is real,
It's inspiration we all feel.

Frederick Elstob (12)
Whitburn CE School, Sunderland

Dream

D emocracy, all should have a say
R acial injustice
E quality for all men, black or white
A ll men should be free
M arch forward from suffering.

Reece Pape (12)
Whitburn CE School, Sunderland

167

Ours . . .

Sitting, listening, seeing, feeling
The waves of the ocean,
Our lives are set into motion,
Questions rupture the silent mind,
All the ones we left behind;
Yet waiting for the ones we have yet to meet,
Finding our balance on steady feet.

Rushing, hastening, hurrying, quickening,
And for what?
Are we all part of one big plot
Or do we choose our own fate
And by what untold date?

Finding, discovering, uncovering, exposing
Our true selves in a crowded world;
Rather than just sitting, just curled,
Trying to reach our expectations,
Jumping up like animations.

Who dictatorially designs? Who gets to decide?
Who lives or dies or stays by your side?
Following or followed?
Individuality is what lets us thrive in this world.
Our own future, our own goals, our own story.

Holly Tufts (14)
Whitburn CE School, Sunderland

My Inspiration

The sea is so beautiful,
With peaceful lapping of the waves.
Why can't we all be as peaceful as the sea?
That's what puzzles me.

The views from mountain tops are so calm,
You can see towns, hills and farms.
Why can't we all be as calm as mountains
And just be friends?

The rolling hills are so restful,
They are old and full of secrets.
Why can't we all be at rest like the hills
And offer each other love and kindness?

The trees tower over everything,
But still consider each other equals.
Why can't we think of each other as equals
And have no wars or unhappiness?

Why can't we be as gentle as nature,
So calm and relaxed?
Then this world would be perfect.
That's what inspires me.
This is my dream.

Penny McKelvey (11)
Whitburn CE School, Sunderland

169

I Have A Dream

I'm inspired by a pebble on the beach,
Sitting next to the sea,
You would never give it a second thought,
But it means a lot to me.

Carried by the ocean waters,
Swept beyond the sand,
No time to look behind,
Or say goodbye to the land.

Now its perilous journey begins,
Great dangers it will face,
Passing fish, sharks, whales and rays,
A journey they cannot trace.

For millions of years travelling,
No pause, no stop, no break,
How could anything cope like that?
The thought of it makes you shake.

So next time you pick up a pebble,
Next time you look at the sea,
Just think of what it's been through,
And how much it means to me.

Alice Buhaenko (12)
Whitburn CE School, Sunderland

I Have A Dream

Rebecca Addlington is my inspiration,
I admire her speed and determination.
Her talent had seemed to come out of the blue,
She brought home two medals, no one had a clue.

As I stare out of the window, what's there is a sea,
It's rippling out there just waiting for me.
It reminds me of the place where Addlington swam,
I thought of her talent and the swimmer I am.

As I read this aloud, I find,
The pool with fast swimmers is close in my mind.
There's a gala, Addlington is leading the rest,
She's my inspiration; I'm glad I chose the best.

As the competitors leave the competition,
Rebecca's dream is no longer a mission.
Rebecca Addlington is my inspiration,
I admire her speed and determination.

I have my dream to be a swimmer,
I hope in the Olympics I can be a winner.
I hope I can swim through the water like a spear,
I'm ready for success, I have no fear.

Georgia Hansen (12)
Whitburn CE School, Sunderland

Daydreams

Looking out of the window,
I daydream silently,
Gazing in wonder,
Thinking quietly.

I see waves crashing down,
Slowly eroding rocks,
Like graceful, white horses,
Wearing blue cotton socks.

Questions are considered,
Like what if I had?
Or what if Martians
Abducted my dad?

I think some more
About my own aspirations,
What do I want to do,
With my imagination?

My day's more appealing
When a daydream occurs,
About anything and anyone,
But schoolwork it deters.

Amy McKeever (12)
Whitburn CE School, Sunderland

I Have A Dream

As great as we are,
Could we improve?
Our hopes and our dreams
Could make the world move.

Flowers on cliff tops,
Small white doves fly,
But all of our car fumes
Are making these die.

Our iPods, our mobiles,
Our laptops, our cars,
Why should we enjoy these,
When other people can't.

The lights on our streets
Are shining up high,
And are drowning out
The stars in the sky.

As great as we are,
Could we improve?
Our hopes and our dreams
Could make the world move.

Kate Nixon (13)
Whitburn CE School, Sunderland

173

The Voice

A voice spoke up for what should be,
He taught so others could be free.
He faced injustice, hate and strife,
And therefore had to give his life.

The voice stood tall, stood strong,
Devoting a life to undo all wrong.
Desperately trying to understand,
How to banish all evil from this land.

Speaking of love and of peace,
Children hand in hand; hatred ceased.
He gave people the hope to inspire,
Something for them to desire.

The voice moved a nation's heart and mind,
His heart-warming message perfecting defined.
He stood there, smiling, spreading love,
Was he an angel from above?

The world honours you,
Your dream at last came true,
Martin Luther King.

Kate Greener (15)
Whitburn CE School, Sunderland

174

I Have A Dream:
Words To Change The World

My dream is to become more than I am,
My dream is to change what I am,
My dream is to jump the hurdles in my life,
My dream is to change my life.

With so many changes within my life,
I have so many dreams within my life,
With so many changes within the world,
I have so many dreams in this world.

This could all be over the hills and far away,
This could be nobody's fault,
We should ramble on in the world,
Make a better place for all.

I wish there could be freedom,
I wish we could live all the time,
I wish I could jump the hurdles,
I wish the end wouldn't draw near.

My dreams to change this world!

Callum Ballantine (11)
Whitburn CE School, Sunderland

I Have A Dream

We said goodbye to our crumbling old school
And moved into a new one, I think it's cool.
Our head teacher has a lovely heart,
I thank her for giving me a fresh, new start.

The best rooms have a view of the sea,
Now I have my own locker key.
A huge new school, it seems like Heaven,
I have a long time to enjoy the school,
Because I am in Year 7.

Our new school must have a heart of gold,
It would be described as brave and bold.
This school is one of my greatest inspirations,
Not just for me, but for the whole nation.

The new facilities and great teachers make it fun to learn,
The better grades I set, the more money I will earn.
The new school will help my dream come true,
And when I become a successful doctor,
I will owe it all to you, our new school.

Jae Munday (12)
Whitburn CE School, Sunderland

Clouds

I wish that I was just like a cloud
Drifting along without a care in the world
Just going wherever the breeze takes me
Seeing the world from up above
Floating along with ease
No dreams for the future
And no school or education
Who needs them when I'm just a cloud
Floating alone wherever the breeze takes me?

That's my style.

Jake Collins (12)
Whitburn CE School, Sunderland

Dreams

As the sun sets, the stars arise
My head hits the pillow, I close my eyes
As I dream of what will be
The deaf will hear
The blind will see
And all the clouds will start to clear
Above the mountains the sun appears
Another day will now begin
As I wait to dream again.

As the sun sets, the stars arrive
My head hits the pillow, I close my eyes
As I dream of what will be
The weak are strong
The slaves are free
As I find where I belong
All the dreamers sing their song
Another day will now begin
As I wait to dream again.

Lucie Rowe (11)
Whitburn CE School, Sunderland

Inspiration

I nspired by people all through the day
N othing at all can get in the way
S inging is a passion, not just a game
P eople with talents are never the same
I know it's a dream that many girls have
R eality may hit, although it is sad
A nything can happen, if you give it a go
T ry your chances at a talent show!
I f you don't try, you'll never know
O nly in a hairbrush, not a microphone
N ote that you are never alone.

Hiba Altaii (12)
Whitburn CE School, Sunderland

177

I Have A Dream

I have a dream that no one knows!
My mind is a powerful machine;
It creates patterns and inspires me to do things.
When I dream, the world comes to a standstill
And in a flash it is there, then it's gone.
As I stand beyond my dream, my hair swishes in my face,
Smothering me with many thoughts.
I think about it strongly,
Wondering what I can do to make it come true.
I take my dream,
But is it false or is it true?
Do I live for it and wait, or do I die and let it come true?
Should I start to live it now or never?
But when I come to live it, it is gone with no way back.
What is left now?
Nothing, only a shadow, not even a man.
Who can I tell?
No one!

Sophie Faddy (15)
Whitburn CE School, Sunderland

I Have A Dream

Inspiration is something other people do
But I look at myself and think I can do it too
Looking out of the window thinking what life could bring
I think of the successful people, gold medallists and Martin Luther King

All you need is hope and strength
And you can go that extra length
To change the world with all you do
Be like those people, determined and strong
And with help and care, you will too.

Ellie Patterson (12)
Whitburn CE School, Sunderland

I Have A Dream -
Words To Change The World

I have a dream
That no man is mean,
That there is no war
And there is no hatred,
That everyone is equal,
There are no arguments,
And that every man is free.

I have a dream
That every country would work together,
Work together to stop global warming,
That any man who is ever racist
Gets what he deserves,
And most of all,
That every man is kind and caring to another.

That is my dream!

Nathaniel Nixon (12)
Whitburn CE School, Sunderland

If Only . . .

Everything flew as smoothly as the air
We can't see it but can feel it in our hair
Wouldn't it be great if you discovered a place
That you had time to look around because it's not a race?
Natural disasters aren't so great
Some get bigger as if they inflate
Under the water can lurk danger
To me it's just a great big stranger
Who would guess what causes stress
Staying inside, oh what a guess!
Get outside and watch the world unfold
Then tell the stories that are yet to be told.

Paul Longden (12)
Whitburn CE School, Sunderland

I Have A Dream Poem

I am inspired by lots
Including little lines and dots
Mainly my inspiration is a ball
It makes me feel six foot tall
My friends and family are great all the time
They even encourage me to stay away from crime
Football is my favourite thing
All the players walk about with bling
It is what I want to do when I grow up
I really want to hold the FA Cup
See me on the telly when I commentate
I reflect on my career and think, wow that was great
As Mr King said, 'I have a dream'
I lived it out playing for my favourite team
We won the treble in 2029
I sit and look back with a glass of red wine.

I had a dream.

Anthony Chambers (11)
Whitburn CE School, Sunderland

I Have A Dream

I

H ave
A
V ision.
E verybody is treated fairly

A nd

D iplomacy solves problems, not wars
R ain falls on parched farms
E verywhere
A nd
M oney is given to the poor.

Jonathan Parry (13)
Whitburn CE School, Sunderland

I Have A Dream

Life is what you make it,
Hopes, dreams and more,
So try your best at everything
And you will find an open door.

The paths are long and winding,
They may lead you astray,
But if you keep on trying,
You will soon find a way.

Trials and tribulations
Of life, they're sure to come,
So hold your head up high
And we will unite as one.

So the moral of this poem is,
Try your best, be strong and true,
Hard work and determination,
Will always pull you through.

Jessica Lynn (12)
Whitburn CE School, Sunderland

I Have A Dream

I magine

H appy
A nimals
V ision
E ating

A nd

D ancing
R ound
E njoying
A
M ouse.

Daniel Cooper (13)
Whitburn CE School, Sunderland

181

The Horizon

The sea is full of life and can be
A source of life for many a family.
It gives willingly from its mysterious deep
And guides us with roadways to land unseen.

Its peaceful waters, calm, azure,
Give comfort to those who are unsure.
Mermaids, dolphins, pirates, sharks,
Light children's eyes with unending sparks.

But the sea can also crash with thunder,
Poseidon's rage can tear asunder,
Ships that stray into churning seas
May not return, despite their pleas.

Unlike the sea, we can choose
To be cruel or kind, to gain or lose,
Friendships and ultimately happiness too.
The decision's in your hands. What will you choose?

Melissa Young (15)
Whitburn CE School, Sunderland

I Had A Dream . . .

If only the world was a mountain view,
Spreading right in front of you,
Inspiring those to change their mind
And leave the dreads and fears behind.

Sports stars Ronaldo and Gerrard too,
Who kept on going until they broke through,
If only I could be like those,
Who have never said, 'stop' or 'no'!

But I can't leave who I really am behind,
I need to push on and start to climb
Up the path towards success
And never stop to catch my breath.

If only the world was a mountain view,
Spreading right in front of you,
The path ahead is clear for me,
Being the best that I can be.

John Campbell (12)
Whitburn CE School, Sunderland

I Have A Dream

I have a dream,
That if all mankind work together
The world will be better forever.
That all of mankind can live in peace
Global warming, this horror must cease.

I don't want to see this world just die
Without fish to swim and birds to fly.
No air to breathe no water to drink
Climate change will make our homeland sink.

We have a dream,
That we will put an end to this evil
From the elephant to the weevil,
All of these creatures will sadly die
They will die in the blink of an eye.
Climate change, for that's its dreadful name
Destroying our planet that's its game.

Daniel Hern (13)
Whitburn CE School, Sunderland

I Have A Dream

I have a dream . . .
I have a dream that all racial conflicts will end.
I have a dream that all young children will come together and be friends.
I have a dream that all crime will stop.
I have a dream that rape and war will be a thing of the past.
I have a dream the world will stay clean.
This is my dream and one day I hope it won't be just a dream!

Melissa Batey (12)
Whitburn CE School, Sunderland

Dirt, Water, Air, Life

You are the fire inside of me,
That flies me high when I am low
And is always there for me no matter,
Through life and death this would not stop.
You have never stopped to doubt my words and actions
And always see light for me at the end of the tunnel,
You have been my ears when I could not hear
And my mouth when I could not speak,
And though it pains you to see me grow, you have to let me go.
Though I will always be there,
When you think you're alone and your world you spent
Years building, comes crashing down upon you,
I will be there pulling you out,
And rebuilding it brick by brick and stone by stone,
Even to the last lick of paint.
I will be there.

Stefan Hetherington (14)
Whitburn CE School, Sunderland

I Have A Dream

I am inspired by many footballers,
Cristiano Ronaldo to be exact!
The way he swerves that ball into the back of the net
Is totally unreal.

He is out of this world at what he does!
I look up to this genius because he inspires me a lot.

When I'm older I want to be like him.
I would not be as arrogant, but as good.

When he is in attack, he is as sharp as a knife,
He does fast tricks like a juggler with the ball.
His shot is like a rocket, which could break down any wall!

One word to describe him is *outstanding!*

Jack Dixon (12)
Whitburn CE School, Sunderland

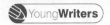

Imagine The Universe

Imagine
Amongst the stars of the universe
All that is yet to know

Imagine
Amongst the galaxies of the universe
All the places still to go

Imagine
Amongst the planets and moons of the universe
Life just like ours

Imagine
Amongst the dust of the universe
Many more meteor showers

Imagine
What we do not know.

Jack Haydock (12)
Whitburn CE School, Sunderland

I Have A Dream

I have a dream, that
When I am older I will be successful in what I do.

I have a dream, that
The world will be peaceful with no wars.

I have a dream, that
In 20 years I will still be in touch with all my friends from school.

I have a dream, that
There will be no sickness or suffering to those who do not deserve it.

I have a dream, that
Everyone will be happy and try in everything they do.

These are my dreams.

Laura Knighton (12)
Whitburn CE School, Sunderland

Ambition

If you want something bad enough
To go out and fight for it
To give up your time and sleep for it

If life seems useless and empty without it
And all you dream about is it
If you'll gladly sweat for it
And bet, fret for it

If you'll simply go after it
With all your capacity
Strength and sagacity
Faith, hope and confidence

If cold, poverty, pain or sickness
Cannot turn you away from the thing you want

You'll get it.

Alex Winship (15)
Whitburn CE School, Sunderland

The Starlight Symphony

I am inspired by the stars above,
In the sky they twinkle, as delicate as love.
They are all unique in their own different way,
The stars are our loved ones, as some people say.

Stars are like humans, they have their own smile,
They light up the evening, they have their own style.
They glisten in the sea, their reflections a glimmer,
Shooting stars leave trails of a dusty, white shimmer.

Stars do not only light up the sky,
They light up my face, as I walk on by.
The stars are like music, each twinkle a note,
Playing a symphony, whilst staying afloat.

Jayden Blacklock (12)
Whitburn CE School, Sunderland

187

He Had A Dream

(In memory of Martin Luther King)

He had a dream,
That one day he would see
The world living in perfect harmony.
Well, now this dream is coming true,
This is all down to me and you.

He did not live to see this day,
Where his children could laugh and play,
The world now is how he wanted,
But some are still disappointed and daunted.
This is my dream, for his to live on,
To listen peacefully to the lark's song.
The whole world now lives as one,
I hope that our dream will live on.

Eliza McNamara (12)
Whitburn CE School, Sunderland

I Have A Dream

I am inspired by footballers,
David Beckham to be exact,
The way he swerves the ball,
He's the best and that's a fact.

He's not like other players,
He's not in it for the money,
He never stops going,
That's what I think is funny.

His determination,
Is so inspiring to me,
And that's why my favourite footballer,
Is Mr David B.

Ben Algie (12)
Whitburn CE School, Sunderland

My Inspiration

I look out the window and I see the dark blue sea,
It inspires me to write on.
Like the mighty force of the ocean hitting the bay
And never stopping.
My ambition is rolling like the white horses prancing up the beach
On the crispy, yellow sand.
I admire its freedom to go wherever it wants,
Like my imagination.
When you are imagining your future,
The sky is the limit.
Imagine a world without limits.
When the waves hit the pier, they leap over,
Showing me that when you dream, boundaries are easily overcome.
I look out of the window and I see the dark blue sea,
It inspires me to dream.

Thomas West (12)
Whitburn CE School, Sunderland

I Have A Dream

I have a dream
That if I believe in myself
Anything is possible

Some of the people that inspire me
To make my dreams come true are
My sporting hero Andrew Flintoff
Who never surrendered his dream
My family who always offer support
And my friends who encourage me

Don't be afraid of high hopes
Work hard
If you don't go after your dreams
You will never achieve
Your goal.

Gareth Welsh (12)
Whitburn CE School, Sunderland

Inspiration

I will remember for years to come
That day the new school was done,
Lots of thoughts went through my head
Whilst I was in my bed.
The old school was great,
The old school was fun,
But I am glad that the new school is done.

And now,
Another four years have gone so fast,
Bucket loads of memories will always last.
I have been given loads of inspiration
And I feel my life will be a sensation.

I will remember for years to come
That day the new school was done.

Emily Hamilton (12)
Whitburn CE School, Sunderland

Young Writers Information

We hope you have enjoyed reading this book - and that you will continue to enjoy it in the coming years.

If you like reading and writing poetry drop us a line, or give us a call, and we'll send you a free information pack.

Alternatively if you would like to order further copies of this book or any of our other titles, then please give us a call or log onto our website at www.youngwriters.co.uk

Young Writers Information
Remus House
Coltsfoot Drive
Peterborough
PE2 9JX
(01733) 890066